"I used these ideas in class and had a wonderful day with my students."

Thank you so much!! I used these ideas in class and had a wonderful day with my students. As a first Year Relief Teacher I find this site invaluable in helping me become a better and more confident Teacher.

Jess (Take Control of the Noisy Class customer)

*   *   *

"It is very rewarding to see a teacher apply strategies from Rob's materials, then get excited as they see the 'magic' work."

"The materials have been right on target, students have benefitted as well as teachers. It is very rewarding to see a teacher apply strategies from Rob's materials, then get excited as they see the 'magic' work. Thank you for making my job easier and validating the experience."

Cheryl E. Le Fon (Take Control of the Noisy Class customer)

Motivate The Unmotivated

A Step-by-Step System You Can Use To Raise Motivation In Your Classroom Tomorrow

Rob Plevin

http://www.needsfocusedteaching.com

About the Author

Rob Plevin is an ex-deputy head teacher and Special Education Teacher with the practical experience to help teachers in today's toughest classrooms.

No stranger to behaviour management issues, Rob was 'asked to leave' school as a teenager. Despite his rocky route through the education system he managed to follow his dream of becoming a teacher after spending several years working as an outdoor instructor, corporate trainer and youth worker for young people in crisis. Since then he has worked with challenging young people in residential settings, care units and tough schools and was most recently employed as Deputy Head at a PRU for children and teenagers with behaviour problems. He was identified as a key player in the team which turned the unit round from 'Special Measures'.

He now runs needsfocusedteaching.com, is the author of several books and presents training courses internationally for teachers, lecturers, parents and care workers on behaviour management & motivation. His live courses are frequently described as 'unforgettable' and he was rated as an 'outstanding' teacher by the UK's Office for Standards in Education.

Rob's courses and resources feature the Needs-Focused Approach™ – a very effective system for preventing and dealing with behaviour problems in which positive staff/student relationships are given highest priority.

To book Rob for INSET or to enquire about live training please visit the help desk at

www.needsfocusedteaching.com

Free bonus materials

Your assignments & checklists

This book is for teachers like you who want fast-acting strategies to create conditions which encourage and stimulate student motivation and engagement. To help you do this, it comes complete with a set of assignments and checklists to help you apply the suggestions and make positive changes in the shortest possible time.

To access these additional resources please visit:

http://needsfocusedteaching.com/kindle/motivate

Introduction

I bet you've had enough. My guess is that you are pretty fed up having to continually 'gee up' and cajole your students into doing their work in your lesson, of trying to make your lessons fun, and of trying to be their friend. You know at times that it can drain you; having to force that smile and be the only source of energy and enthusiasm in the classroom.

Or perhaps you're not a cajoler. You could equally be fed up having to be constantly 'on top' of your students – issuing warning after warning, moving disruptive students to the front of the room, giving detentions, sending them to senior staff, sending notes home, keeping them back after the lesson and waiting... and waiting... for coursework/homework, indeed any work, to be handed in.

Don't worry. You are not alone. Some years ago I conducted a survey (completed by several hundred teachers at all levels from primary up to Post-16) on my website about motivation in the classroom and it turns out that it's a very common problem.

Working on the results of the survey I identified ten main problems associated with low motivation among students. These are the problems which hundreds of teachers identified so there is a good chance these are problems that you face with your students too, whatever age-group you teach.

Problem #1: They have no interest in the lesson activity

Problem #2: They are noisy and disruptive

Problem #3: They flatly refuse to comply

Problem #4: They chatter constantly

Problem #5: They have negative attitudes which effect other students

Problem #6: Their punctuality is poor

Problem #7: They just won't complete work in class

Problem # 8: There is a 'joker' – that one student who disrupts the group

Problem # 9: They don't hand in homework

Problem # 10: They don't bring equipment to class

... and that's just the top ten. Do you experience any of them? A few of them? Perhaps even all of them?

Now, think for a minute how it would be if you had answers for some or all of these ten main problems? How would your day be, for example, if you knew the specific steps to put in place to prevent students from arriving late to class without their homework, without a pen, intent on wrecking your lesson?

How would it be if you had a simple system for changing the attitudes of your students, for example, so that they started arriving (on time) at your classroom door with a smile, eager to get in the room and start the activities? Stop laughing; it really can happen!

Imagine how you'd feel getting up in the morning without the usual dread but the skills and knowledge to deal confidently with the few students who will try to disrupt your lesson. It would be great wouldn't it? Now think about the students and how they would feel if their grades were going up and they could finally see a point in the stuff you're constantly fighting over.

This is all possible. You really can change the attitudes of your students; you really can get them interested. And it's easier than you think. I've trained thousands of teachers to do this and if they have managed it, you can too.

Although there is no single magical, one-size-fits-all formula for motivating all your students all the time, there are certain general factors which if included in lessons, can give you the best possible chances of engaging most of your students, most of the time. That's a runner-up prize not to be sneezed at.

This book, combined with the program of action it includes, is going to help you get over the student motivation hurdles you're currently facing. By the time you complete it I'm confident that you really will see a significant improvement in the motivation of most, if not all, your students. You will have set in place a new system for improving attitudes and you will have the strategies and skills to deal with problems together with a handy set of reminders to help you stick to them. I won't promise that changes will happen overnight but, as long as you actually implement the suggestions, in a week or two from now things will get a lot easier.

To begin our journey into raising the motivation of our students let's first start by examining why they're NOT currently motivated.

Why Your Students Are Unmotivated

I have listed below four possible reasons why your students might be currently unmotivated. This list isn't exclusive but being aware of these particular de-motivators is important because they are incredibly wearing and will counteract even the most powerful and ingenious motivation strategies. The extent to which these de-motivators are reduced will dictate how successful our motivating strategies will be when we come to put them in place – the two go hand in hand.

Reason #1: RELEVANCE - They don't see any relevance in what is being taught.

Responsible students and those who have a positive family and parental influence work hard in school because they know the value and importance of education and its necessity for success in life. But many of our students simply don't see a connection between school and real life.

"What's the point in this sir?" and *"Why do we have to do this?"* are the more polite ways a student might complain about the relevancy of a lesson on trigonometry, but if their complaints stop at that level you're very lucky. Bored, frustrated students who see no point in the work usually become a major disruption in lessons.

Reason #2: FEAR - They fear failure and embarrassment.

Fear is a crippling emotion. It prevents us from taking risks such as putting a hand up to answer a question in front of 'clever' peers, and therefore keeps us from growing and learning. How can you stretch out and try new things if you're crippled by fear and don't want to look foolish?

On my live courses I often introduce the idea that everyone present will have to get up on stage at some point during the day to either take part in a role play or do something to entertain the rest of the group. It doesn't go down well with some people – particularly the shy ones, or those who have left their banjo at home.

Frequently I watch as they mutter to each other "we don't have to do this" and "I am NOT doing that!" – very similar comments to those made by students who are given work they don't 'like'. The look of sheer horror on some of the participants' faces at the mere mention of 'role play' is priceless.

But after enjoying seeing them squirm for a few moments I smile and say "Don't worry, I won't ask you to come up to the front unless you want to. But you might like to think about this for a moment...

...how many times do you present your students with tasks about which they are probably equally fearful?"

When I was in primary school I developed an incredible fear of reading aloud in class (and vacuum cleaners, but that's another story). My fear was so profound that I used to shake and stammer uncontrollably. The terror I experienced had such a hold on me that I was unable to speak at all – I would try but the words just wouldn't come out and I would be reduced to a bright red, teary-eyed terror-stricken mute.

By the time I reached secondary school this fear was so entrenched that I avoided all requests to read out in class at all costs. I avoided Wednesday's English lessons for a whole year because that was the day we did group reading. Half my English lessons that year were spent hiding in the toilets with the other skivers. (Which could explain the high percentage of typos in my marketing materials!)

I should point out that I wasn't a wallflower at school. Far from it. Many teachers considered me to be something of a clown – outspoken, cheeky and lively with size 20 boots - which made my deep fear of reading aloud all the more confusing to me and also to my friends. How could a normally gregarious big lad be so self-conscious and fearful when it came to reading out loud?

I never did find the reasons behind my fear of public speaking (although the way I got over it is a subject for another time) but I did learn something incredibly important for my teaching career: fear is one of the main reasons for work avoidance among students.

Think how you feel when you're asked to do something outside your comfort zone, and remember that the fierce arguments, bold complaints and other seemingly offensive or vindictive actions from some students may simply be a means to conceal the real reason they appear unmotivated: fear of embarrassment, ridicule, criticism or failure.

Reason #3: INADEQUACY - They feel inadequate.

School is a miserable and frustrating experience for many students (and teachers come to think of it!). By the time they reach 11 or 12 students who have experienced failure almost every day for years have a clear image in their heads that they can't learn. School has become somewhere they struggle and they see no light on the horizon.

They see other students doing quite nicely, producing lovely pieces of artwork, writing neatly, understanding concepts, answering questions etc, whereas they simply fail every day.

Their work is messy, they can't keep up. Sometimes they get a glimmer of success when a friendly teacher congratulates them for a single piece of work but their image of themselves as a failure is so entrenched that they quickly revert back to the comfortable and known feeling of themselves as a failure.

Well, would you feel motivated to learn a new concept if you'd had experiences like that? Would you turn up for class with an eager smile on your face?

Reason #4: UNINSPIRING WORK – They expect to be bored.

Some lesson topics are B-O-R-I-N-G. There's just no getting away from it. Teachers have limited time and resources and can't possibly make every lesson a big hit with their students. Now and again you can be forgiven for having a lesson of bookwork or worksheets. Now and again you can be forgiven for a lack-lustre performance and for not displaying your usual enthusiasm and love for your subject. No problem there, that's life.

The problems arise when the majority of lessons all follow the same format. If there is a continual lack of challenge, a continual lack of variety and a continual lack of novelty there will almost certainly be a continual lack of interest from the students.

When was the last time you put the television on and sat through a really boring film on your own? You just wouldn't would you? If it wasn't to your satisfaction you would just turn it off (even if Nicholas Cage isn't in it).

Students don't have the luxury of being able to 'change channels' to a more interesting lesson or teacher. This is why their boredom comes out as disruption, defiance or avoidance.

It may be because the work is too easy (not enough challenge), too difficult (makes them switch off), has zero activity or interaction built in, has no relevance (see #1) or because they've simply been working too long without a break.

So these are our main 'de-motivators'. At this stage we just need to be aware that they exist and that they have an impact on how our students feel. As we get further into the program we will implement strategies to reduce these factors but for now let's take a look at another area which isn't going to help us if we are to increase our students' motivation levels. Before we can put our Motivating the Unmotivated System in place we have to rid ourselves of the...cue the wolf howls and full moon...

Motivation Myths – beliefs which WON'T help

Myth #1: Some students are beyond help – they simply aren't motivated by anything.

Even the child who drags his heels everywhere he goes and seems uninterested in anything at all is motivated by something. At the very least he must be motivated by food otherwise he'd be dead. Perhaps it's playing football with his mates, the prospect of building a den or the opportunity to see his favourite band in concert. He's just not motivated to do what you want him to when you want him to do it!

When they won't take part in your quiz it's not that they're unmotivated, it's because they are motivated not to take part in your quiz – something else has a bigger pull for them than the quiz. Incredible but true.

Myth #2: Competition is a motivator

A lot of teachers in the UK may have watched (and been impressed by) the wonderful Gareth Malone and his 'Extraordinary School for Boys' (2011). There were some fantastic ideas in this programme and while I love Mr Malone's passion and creativity, I do disagree with one of the things the programme focused on:

...competition is not a panacea when it comes to increasing motivation.

I disagree for one reason – The only person who is truly motivated by a competition is a person who believes he has a fair chance of winning.

Our classrooms are inclusive and whether you agree with inclusion or not, it is with us for the foreseeable future. Competitive activities – games, quizzes, puzzles, tests, projects, fist-fights etc. can be terrific motivators – but only when ALL students have an equal chance of winning. In an inclusive classroom this is not the case. The only person who is truly motivated by a competition is a person who believes he has a fair chance of winning and obviously, this is not the case for a proportion of students in every classroom.

As we've already discovered, those who aren't motivated to take part in an activity (because of perceived weakness and inability to compete on an equal footing) are going to be motivated not to take part- or to take part and disrupt.

I'm not saying quizzes and games have no place in the classroom – they do – but care has to be taken to either base them on non-academic strengths as a purely 'fun' exercise in which all students have an equal chance, or to ensure students are split into diverse learning teams* so that all students feel they have an equal chance through peer support.

*'Diverse Learning Teams' will be fully explained in the 'Strategies for Meeting the Need to Belong' section later in this programme.

Myth #3: It's not my job to motivate these kids. They are here to learn – I shouldn't have to make learning fun just to get them to work!

I've been told this on many occasions when delivering live courses by teachers who hold the belief that if students can't be bothered or are too stupid to take the opportunity to learn, then it is their loss, it's their problem.

"I'm a teacher, not a circus clown!" was the reply once when I suggested adding a little fun and humour in his lessons to a teacher - who was, I discovered later, uniformly hated by his students.

These are the teachers who sit at the back of the training room, arms folded, deep frown, eyes rolling to the ceiling, sighing audibly at salient points and frequently turning their backs and talking to their neighbours. Yes, it's rude, but it makes me smile. The behaviour they display is tellingly similar to the very behaviour they complain about so fiercely in their students!

I can give reason after reason why it is so crucially beneficial for the teacher to stretch out and connect with the students who don't want to learn – from the student's point of view. If we don't prepare them for life, who will? It's not their fault if their parents have given them a bad start and prepared them for nothing more than dialling for a pizza from the comfort of the couch when commercials interrupt the X Factor. In our crumbling society with its tumbling social values do we want to be part of the solution or part of the problem?

Those arguments, although valid and worthwhile, seldom change the mind of a staunch disbeliever. Set in their ways, they're tough nuts to crack so I switch the focus over to them. What's in it for them? It's a good question to ask if you want to motivate anyone.

The rewards are many and great for the teacher who connects with the most challenging, disinterested students. As many will testify, getting it right with a difficult student can turn out to be the most rewarding moment in any teaching career. Who wouldn't like to look back on their years and say that they truly changed a child's life for the better? If you got a call from an ex-student ten years after they'd left school and they told you what an amazing influence you had on their formative years – forgive the sentimentality but you'd have to be made of stone not to be moved, wouldn't you?

The benefits to teachers aren't limited to the 'feel-good' factor; from a purely selfish point of view, it makes your job easier and more pleasant. Stress – from constant battles with challenging individuals and groups - is one of the main reasons teachers are leaving the profession in droves. When you have the students on your side these stresses are reduced. You have more time, and you have a better time.

At the end of the day, however, it's a matter of personal opinion. Some people feel a teacher's job is to prepare young people for life and all aspects of it. Others believe their influence stops at academic tutoring alone and need go no further than the last page of the course books. Regardless of personal opinion the question facing every teacher remains:

What are you going to do with the students who aren't motivated?

You still have to teach them, whether it's your job to motivate them or not. Better find a way to get them motivated quick... all other things considered, low grades don't look good!

Myth #4: Carrots are terrific motivators

Motivating your students is actually not that hard to achieve. Let's face it, a suitably attractive reward can work wonders, can't it? Offer a group of teenagers £10 to pick up litter after the lesson and volunteers will be falling over themselves, right? There you go, Student Motivation Made Simple – just give them a cash reward.

There's a problem with rewards though, even a pile of cash. They are only really effective for low order tasks requiring little or no creative thought. Offer the same £10 reward in return for a piece of creative writing and you'll get a much different result.

Some students, those who enjoy thinking of stories and are capable writers for example, may well put their hearts and souls into the task. But those who prefer to flick bogeys during English lessons, while interested enough in the promise of £10 to put pen to paper, probably won't manage the sustained effort and thought necessary to produce their 'best ever' piece of work.

Besides, the effectiveness of rewards wears out over time. It's not that rewards and incentives can't effect change, they can, and we'll be looking at ways to use them effectively later in the program. Some individuals, particularly younger children and students with behaviour issues and limited emotional skills, benefit from having good behaviour reinforced.

But care should be taken so that they don't become relied upon. Students who become conditioned to expect rewards feel entitled to receiving more and more. "Okay, I'll do as you say, but what are you going to give me in return?" is the stock response. Next time it becomes "Okay, I'll do what you want again, but I want something better this time."

Sadly, we are developing a society of young people who have a permanently outstretched arm from being promised reward after reward, both at home and at school, as a short term method to getting them quiet, 'on side' and motivated to do what we want them to.

Myth #5: Get the big stick out – that'll get them working

What about punishments? If they can't be coerced or bribed into a doing a task with a fat, juicy reward, surely your students can be browbeaten with a sufficiently threatening penalty? Well, yes and no. Some can, but the students who do fear threats and punishments are those who usually conform. The hard cases have heard it all before and couldn't care less; it's water off a duck's back.

Again, in the short term, with some students (usually the less problematic ones) it does work, there's no doubt about it. But is the negativity, fear and avoidance that this route generates conducive to positive student-teacher relationships and long term motivation? Not usually.

Rewards, punishments and external control methods are 'quick fixes'. The main problem with them is that once one of these strategies wears out, you have to go in search of another. It's a lot like eating sugary snacks – you get brief highs followed by empty lows. Attempts to control students in this way can only ever give, at best, short term bursts of motivation.

So, if these strategies don't work just how do you motivate a student who simply **does not care?** How do you motivate a student who is totally **opposed to learning?** How do you motivate students who are **apathetic, lazy, disinterested and** - perhaps worst of all - **disruptive**?

Well, rather than trying to artificially pump motivation into students from the outside, let's do it properly. Let's focus on the right TYPE of motivation... real motivation, intrinsic motivation that is generated from within.

Motivating students from the inside out

We are all born with our motivation button having been fully pre-pressed. Watch any young child and you will see natural, internal motivation in action – they want to discover, they need to explore, they absolutely must touch, taste, push, pull. They don't need to be bribed or coerced into learning more about something new. There is no need for rewards or threats because their motivation is intrinsic, it comes from inside, driven by a desire to learn.

As we get older that natural drive to learn for learning's sake is dampened. Other factors come into play. We no longer have the freedom to be interested in what we want to be interested in - certainly not all the time. Learning something for the sake of learning – and for the natural joy and sense of discovery involved - more commonly becomes 'learning to achieve a certain grade', to get moved into a higher set or to avoid being kept in at play time. And this is when the problems start; this is when teachers buy into the Motivation Myths described above in an attempt to control students and make them motivated.

We know it doesn't work. So let's forget the myths and stick with the kind of internal motivation that has students engaged and involved for the enjoyment of the task itself – not because they are trying to earn a merit mark or avoid a detention.

OK, how do we do it?

"Desire is the key to motivation"

Mario Andretti

It's not hard to see that desires have a lot to do with raising real motivation in the classroom because the only way a person will be truly motivated to do something is if they actually want to do it. But where does this desire come from and how can we, as teachers, tap into it and create a situation in which our students want to take part?

The answer to this perplexing question... and the secret to increasing intrinsic motivation in the classroom, (get this right and you'll never need to resort to carrots and sticks again), lies in...

...providing a learning environment in which your students' key psychological needs are being met.

Definition: 'Need'

To most psychologists, a need is a feature that arouses an organism to action toward a goal, giving purpose and direction to behaviour.

Our needs are crucial to human motivation – they cause us to do what we do, they make behaviour happen. At a very basic level, for example, we all have a need for food and it's that need which drives us to get off the sofa, make a sandwich and eat it. If we weren't able to find food this need would not be met and we'd end up becoming fashion models. Eventually, of course, we'd starve to death.

That's an extreme example involving our most basic 'survival needs'. Missing out on a 'psychological need' isn't likely to result in death but it would have a significant effect on our overall sense of wellbeing. Satisfaction of our psychological needs is vitally important if we are to feel content and fulfilled and has as much, if not more, influence over our behaviour.

As you know, this theory is not new (although the fashion model bit is a late addition). The theory of needs-driven motivation was first proposed by Abraham Maslow and is supported by many psychologists including Professor David McClellan in "The Achieving Society" and Dr William Glasser in "Choice Theory". The idea being, that people are intrinsically motivated to continually try to meet one or more of the psychological needs which form part of their genetic structure.

So, which psychological needs in particular are we referring to? Well, there is no definitive list, it depends a lot on which psychologist or theorist you're talking to, but I believe they can be categorised into just three broad groups to keep things nice and simple. These three groups of psychological needs hold the key to raising levels of intrinsic motivation in your classroom...

1. The need for **Belonging**; the need to love and be loved, to be appreciated, valued, needed and connected.

2. The need for **Empowerment**; the need to feel competent, to succeed & achieve (and be recognised for those achievements) as well as being free to make choices & be autonomous.

3. The need for **Fun**; the need for excitement & adventure, variety, amusement, entertainment and surprise.

Not convinced? To highlight how need-satisfaction (in particular, satisfaction of the three groups of needs I've just mentioned) plays a part in motivating your students, let's look at something which holds almost universal appeal for them - particularly unmotivated boys. You guessed it; game consoles.

Every young boy in your class is likely to spend a large slice of his life playing one of these things, and not because he is forced or bribed to, but because he desperately wants to. He might not be able to sit still and concentrate on his work for more than five minutes at a time yet he will happily sit for hours on end playing a computer game; often in preference to eating and sleeping.

So what are the features of computer games which make them so appealing? If we could somehow integrate these same features into our lessons, we'd stand a very good job of raising intrinsic motivation, right?

In a study on this issue, psychologists at the University of Rochester asked 1,000 gamers what motivated them to keep playing. The results published in the journal Motivation and Emotion suggested that people enjoy video games **because they find them <u>intrinsically satisfying.</u>** The research found that games can provide opportunities for <u>achievement</u>, <u>freedom</u>, and, in the case of online communities, a <u>connection</u> to other players.

*"We think there's a deeper theory than the **fun** of playing. It's our contention that the psychological 'pull' of games is largely due to their capacity to engender feelings of **autonomy**, **competence**, and **relatedness**."*

Richard M. Ryan, motivational psychologist at the University of Rochester

Did you catch that? According to the researchers, the allure of video games is largely rooted in their capacity engender feelings of <u>autonomy</u> and <u>competence</u> (**empowerment**), <u>relatedness</u> (**belonging**) and, of course, **fun**. (Nobody could argue that users don't have fun when they play).

So, hopefully you'll agree that satisfying your students' psychological needs is a fairly dependable way to increase intrinsic motivation. Even if the research on computer games hasn't convinced you, I'm sure you can see that it's basic common sense. We CAN'T get the best from our students through punishment and reward, we have to be smarter than that and the Needs Focused Approach offers a sensible, logical solution.

OK, the theory is all well and good but I know what you really want – practical stuff you can use in your classroom. So how do we go about satisfying these student needs within the constraints of the day-to-day classroom setting?

This is achieved by altering the only areas over which we have direct control, the only things we can fully influence: the lesson delivery/ teaching styles we adopt, the learning environment we create and the activities & tasks we present.

Throughout the rest of 'Motivate The Unmotivated' we will explore creative and effective strategies to meet the three core needs (**Belonging, Power & Fun**) in order to motivate your students from WITHIN.

Assignment 1

It's time for a little assignment. I know you probably don't want to do an assignment now that you've just sat down with a cup of coffee but I'm afraid this isn't a 'buy it, skim through it and stick it on the shelf' book. Well, I don't want it to be, anyway. You've paid good money to solve your student motivation problems but they are only going to change if action is taken. The action starts here with this simple exercise:

1) **Case Studies – Pre-course strategies**: Use your current knowledge and skills to solve the most common motivation problems.

Your Case Studies are in the **online resource area** which accompanies this book. They look like this:

You'll notice that there is a 'PRE-COURSE' section and a 'POST-COURSE' section for each scenario. At this stage, you fill in the **PRE-COURSE** section **only**. Please take a few minutes to look through the scenarios and jot some ideas down as to how you would tackle them.

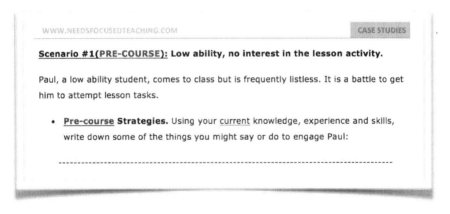

CASE STUDIES

Scenario #1(PRE-COURSE): Low ability, no interest in the lesson activity.

Paul, a low ability student, comes to class but is frequently listless. It is a battle to get him to attempt lesson tasks.

- **Pre-course Strategies.** Using your current knowledge, experience and skills, write down some of the things you might say or do to engage Paul:

You don't have to do it now but it's a good idea to get it out of the way. Then you can have your coffee!

Strategies to Satisfy the Need to Belong

We all share the basic need to belong, and to be made to feel that we do; this is the most important of the 'three needs'.

The main message behind the various courses and resources we provide is that most behaviour problems in school can be effectively prevented by building and maintaining positive student/teacher relationships and by making students feel valued and appreciated. But this message applies equally to motivating students who are faced with difficult tasks or work they see no point in completing - they are more apt to listen to a teacher they trust and respect.

We are going to approach this from two angles:

1. building positive peer relationships within the classroom community, and

2. building positive student/teacher relationships.

Create a COMMUNITY in the classroom

Students are most motivated when they feel they are part of a community in which they feel accepted and in which individuality is encouraged. By definition a community is a group of people who work with one another building a sense of trust, care, and support – kind of like a family. This means that in our classrooms, part of our job is to provide opportunities and structures by which students can work collaboratively and support and help one another. Creating a motivating classroom community which fosters a sense of belonging peacefully does not happen by accident but requires time, persistence and planning. The following ideas will help you do it.

Community Builder #1:

Hold Student Meetings

Meetings with selected students are valuable tools for finding out what is or is not working for them, for handling issues that arise and for seeking ideas about how things can improve. They are also perfect for building bonds with your students and provide opportunity to give positive feedback in a private setting.

Giving your students a voice and involving them in decisions makes them feel more connected and shows you value them; it shows you are there to support them and care sincerely about their progress. These meetings also go a long way to reduce the de-motivators we mentioned earlier in 'Why Your Students are NOT Motivated' because they give them opportunity to talk about their fears and inadequacies, to find relevance in what is being taught and to suggest alternative teaching/learning methods which they may find more inspiring or interesting.

Meetings should be scheduled once a week or once a fortnight with small groups of up to five students, who can be grouped according to their level of motivation/interest. It is a good idea to give the groups a positive label such as 'Solutions Focus Group A' which conveys to them that they have been recruited to help you make improvements for the benefits of the whole class, and that their opinions and ideas are valued.

When you first approach students to be part of a meeting emphasis needs to be placed on the fact that it is for their benefit and that you need their opinions and ideas. This could be done face to face or you could invite them through a written invitation.

The purpose of the meetings is NOT to apportion blame or complain about lack of work, rather it is to solicit ideas from the students about how to make things better and to talk about what is working ("we'll do more of these activities") and what isn't working ("we'll do fewer of these activities or seek to improve them").

Meetings need only be five or ten minutes long – little more than a quick summary of ideas and feedback so can be slotted into any timetable without too much inconvenience.

Community Builder #2:

Give Them Ownership of the Physical Environment

Research suggests that a warm and caring environment improves attendance and motivation and that the more input students have, the better the sense of belonging they gain. Remember:

It is far easier for them to reject and opt out of something they don't feel involved in than it is for them to turn their backs on something they've helped create.

Students can be asked to contribute and get involved in the following ways:

• Create a photo board with pictures taken of the class involved in various activities throughout the term. Younger children, in particular, need to see themselves 'reflected' in the classroom. Invite parents and family members to send in photos of their children and family and create a display with them. Seeing themselves as part of the physical environment will go a long way towards making young children feel comfortable but they will also enjoy learning about their friends' families too.

• Designate a display board as the 'Graffiti Wall'. Put up a background of painted brickwork and give each student the opportunity to define their own name or 'tag' in graffiti lettering and stick them up on the wall. Students of all ages love this activity. You can give them ideas by looking at graffiti samples online and downloading ready-made letter templates in various designs for them to copy.

• Ask them to bring in reading materials or quiet activities so they can read their magazines and play quiet games in free time. If you have the space and resources to have a designated 'quiet area' so much the better.

• Provide a Student Notice Board' on which class members can put up notices, adverts, invitations, certificates, letters, samples of work , photos etc.

• Create a suggestion box for students to come up with ways to make the classroom better.

• Involve them in arranging and decorating the room.

Community Builder # 3:

Bonding Sessions

The benefits of team-building exercises and getting-to-know-you activities in relation to developing peer relationships and classroom community are significant. They provide opportunity for individual students to develop communication skills, appreciate each other's strengths and capabilities and bond with other. Activities can be incorporated into lessons as aids to learning or can be scheduled as one-off lessons or starter activities. Time spent off curriculum on these activities is never wasted and will be paid back in terms of increased motivation, improved morale and better relationships.

I have included a couple of activities below taken from three of my other titles: **The FUN Teachers' Tool Kit, The Active Learning Tool Kit** and '**Attention-Grabbing Starters & Plenaries**' which are all available at reasonable cost through Amazon. These books are jammed with starters, plenaries, fill-ins, ice-breakers, team-builders and games to engage your switched off students. Getting them interested in any activity in the classroom – even one not strictly related to the curriculum - is a tremendous first step in turning around severely disengaged students. Once they see that the classroom can be interesting and enjoyable, you have a foundation for growth and further learning.

Whether you use the ideas in my books or not, it is imperative to have a stock of suitable fun, interactive activities to get students up on their feet and engaged in something they can enjoy and benefit from. I will give you a few more ideas later in the 'Strategies to Satisfy the Need for FUN' section.

52 Card Pick-up

Overview: This team-building activity allows students to experience, first hand, the benefits to be had from cooperating with each other rather than working alone or arguing.

It's hard-hitting yet great fun and ideal for small SEN groups with behaviour or social problems.

Number of people: Small group split into teams of 3-4.

Materials: a pack of playing cards for each team.

Time: 10 minutes.

Directions:

1. Split the group into teams of three or four.

2. Take out the playing cards from the pack, shuffle them and lay them face down on the floor in a mess.

3. Tell the team you are giving them a challenge – simply to gather up all the cards and put them back in order in the pack (Ace through to King for each suit). Let them know you'll be timing them.

4. The team (particularly if it is a group of boys) will almost certainly fall apart and students will argue with each other as they attempt the task as individuals. Record the time taken as soon as they have finished.

5. Ask why it took them so long and if they could suggest ways to improve. How could they work together to get a quicker time? Talk through and help them summarise their suggestions – usually they realise it will be better if they nominate who is going to be responsible for each suit and then agree to pass relevant cards to each other as they

pick them up. They may also suggest working within strict areas instead of everyone trying to pick up all the cards.

6. Repeat the exercise – they will be astounded at how quickly they complete the task this second time by cooperating with each other.

7. Ask each student to reflect on what happened and to state what they've learned.

Sample Team Builder #2:

Save the Egg

Number of people: Any size group.

Materials: EACH GROUP NEEDS: 1 Egg, 15 straws, a roll of masking tape, recyclable plastic bottles, newspaper, rubber bands plus any other insulating-type materials you can find.

Time: One full lesson - 60 minutes (30 to build package, 15 to launch eggs, 15 to clean up and reflect).

Directions:

1. Form teams of 4-5 students.

2. Explain that their task is to create a container which will maintain their egg intact after an 8-foot drop.

3. Give students 30 minutes to create the container.

4. Create a lot of theatrics around the actual Egg Drop. It makes it more fun.

5. Allow each group to wish their egg luck and drop it from the 8-foot mark.

6. Gather the safe eggs and clean up the broken ones and the rest of the mess.

7. Gather to reflect on the eggsperience focusing on how the particular teams worked together.

Variation:

Rather than a device to protect the egg from a fall, groups work to build a device to 'launch' the egg through the air – similar to the ancient Greek weapon, the Ballista, and make it travel as far as they can. I've found this version of the activity to be particularly popular with boys. It also brings some of them out of their shells.

Community Builder # 4:

Cooperative Group Work

By setting up cooperative learning activities for your students you actually meet all three needs – Belonging, Power & Fun - which makes this a very effective strategy for increasing motivation in lessons.

Positive peer relationships are developed as a result of students helping each other to reach a common goal. Attention-seeking students are no longer alone; attention is being received from their fellow group members so there is less incentive to disrupt. Lower-achieving students also benefit by gaining confidence and motivation by working together with the higher achieving students. Higher-achieving students also benefit by helping and guiding the lower-achievers by reinforcing their understanding of the material. Social skills such as self-expression, decision making abilities, collaboration, problem solving, responsibility, sharing, listening, and conflict management are all naturally developed.

There is a hidden benefit too - cooperative & active learning activities SAVE YOU TIME. In many cases, once your students are used to the frameworks, they effectively teach themselves. Suddenly you are free from constant requests for attention and can actually enjoy giving quality support when it is required rather than when it's demanded.

There are many ways to group students when you're preparing an activity and different types of groupings have different benefits and disadvantages. In some cases it might be suitable to allow students to pick their own groups but generally it will be up to the teacher to decide which groupings work best for the class and for particular projects. Groupings should be rotated and changed regularly so that the whole class group interacts and does not degenerate into cliques.

Grouping Type #1:

Random Groups

This is the quickest way to form groups and is best suited to either 'fun' sessions where the mix of individuals is not so important, or new groups of individuals you don't yet know particularly well. Like 'friendship' groups (where students are simply told to get together in a group with their friends), students see this as a 'fair' way to be grouped, as it is based on chance rather than a deliberate choice made by the teacher. As you get to know your students you will naturally find that grouping some individuals together is not appropriate, and you will gradually move away from 'random groupings' to more planned and organised methods explained below.

Ideas for forming 'Random Groups':

1. Pull the names out of a hat

2. Stick pins in the register

3. Number round the class

Numbering the class is a very quick and easy way of forming random groups and there is potential for sub-grouping part-way through an activity if necessary; eg start by counting the class off in fours and have each 'group of four' work together for the first activity. Have the class regroup later by putting all the ones together in one group, all the twos together in another group, and so on.

4. Comic Strips

Cut cartoon strips into separate frames – one strip for each group. If you want to form six groups, you need six different cartoon strips, perhaps taking each from one comic. For example, The Beano would provide strips such as Minnie the Minx, Dennis the Menace, Roger the Dodger etc.

The frames from strips are mixed up and one frame is given to each pupil as they enter the room. They then have to find other members from the same cartoon to form their 'strip'.

5. Puzzles

Simple jigsaw puzzles can be made by sticking pictures from magazines on to cardboard and then cutting the picture up to your desired shape, size and number of pieces; a slightly more expensive but quicker way is to visit a toy shop. You want large simple puzzles – the type for very young children if you're buying them – with five or six pieces.

You need the same number of puzzles as groups you're trying to create – ie, if you want to split the class into six groups of five, you need six puzzles, each with at least five pieces.

Mix up the pieces from all the puzzles and give each student a puzzle piece. When you are ready to form the students into groups, put some music on and instruct them to find others with pieces from their puzzle. The groups should sit down with their completed puzzles in front of them.

Note: If you want to get really clever you can source pictures which have a link to the lesson content and use these as prompts for starter questions.

TIP: If you want your sub-groups to form with minimum disruption and confusion deal with them in stages and get them to identify themselves to each other. Simply telling all the 'ones' to get together will cause chaos because nobody knows who all the 'ones' are – they will be shouting out to each other to try and identify the right group. You can eliminate this problem very easily:

"All the ones raise your right hand. Keep your hand raised until you are in a group of four ones. Once you have found three other number ones, put your hands down and sit down in your new group."

Give them a few minutes and then go through the other teams.

Grouping Type #2:

Mixed-Skills Groups

This is where students with different skills or strengths are grouped together. Each group might have, for example, a note-taker with neat hand-writing, a natural leader who acts as motivator, a talented artist, and a confident presenter. Students then naturally fall into a role that benefits their group.

Some teachers like to assign roles within groups, helping students along and sometimes challenging students with roles that they wouldn't necessarily have chosen. As the teacher, you can assign roles by handing out cards for various roles, such as "note-taker," "reporter", "presenter", "motivator," "artist," etc. This is a helpful way to approach mixed-skills groups in classrooms that are particularly rowdy, or with students who aren't familiar with group work and wouldn't necessarily know how to assign roles themselves. This grouping helps motivate individuals because everyone has an important part to play in their group's success – it relies on peer encouragement.

Grouping Type #3:

Similar-skills groups

Students with similar skills and strengths are grouped together. This is more effective if you are working on a large class project - each small group can then focus on just one aspect of that project.   If you are producing a play, for example, you could have a group of artistic students responsible for the scenery; a group of creative and active students responsible for finding costumes; and a group of writers responsible for perfecting the script.

This type of group doesn't work for all projects, since group assignments usually involve various tasks that require different skills. The one major benefit from this type of group, though, is that students are motivated because they get to do what they are good at so it helps motivate individuals because they get to develop (or 'show off') their skills in an area they already enjoy.

Grouping Type #4:

Same Interest Groups

Like similar-skills groups, same interest groups only work for certain projects. They are especially effective for research projects, where students who are interested in researching a specific topic can work together. When preparing for this type of group, it helps to have students write down their top three choices (of research topics or other topics that will determine their groups) on a card. This works best if you present the topics and have students immediately write down their choices, so they don't get to discuss topics with their friends and agree to write only what their friends are writing.

The students' choices determine their groups (though you may have to intervene if you know that certain groupings won't work – this is one reason why you should have students write several choices on their cards). If, for example, the class has been studying mediaeval Europe, you might end up with one group focusing on knights, one on castles, one on medicine, and one on dragons the daily life of serfs. It is then up to you to decide how you want students to do this research.

Are they each going to do their own research, with the group just there to help problem-solve? Or is each group going to present one project, with each member focusing on one aspect of the project? In this case, you may also find it useful to assign individual roles in the group so students can complete the project effectively. This grouping helps motivate individuals because they get to work with, and bounce ideas off, those with similar interests.

Grouping Type #5:

Performance Groups

In this type, the teacher groups students together by current levels of performance in a certain subject, so that students who want to move faster can do so with their group, and students who need more time can take that time in a slower one. This is an ideal way for a language-arts teacher to assign various books in a class of widely varying abilities. The teacher can group by reading ability and then assign appropriate books to each group. This works best when the teacher also assigns tasks for the group to complete as they read; maybe they have to find five vocabulary words in each chapter, create and answer ten reading questions for each chapter, or design a poster to teach the rest of the class about the book. For younger students, each group could have their own spelling list, so that good spellers can move ahead more quickly than those who struggle with it. This method helps motivate individuals because students get to move at a pace that works for them – faster workers won't get bored while less able students don't get so frustrated or feel left behind.

Grouping Type #6:

Support/Mixed Ability Groups

In this type we group one or two students who are strong in a subject with one or two students who need support in that subject. This method can cause some students to feel (and act) superior and others to feel second class, so you need to be careful how you use this grouping.

It's crucial for the teacher to convey the idea that those needing support are not inferior in any way, but would benefit from some support in a particular area. If teachers can group students in such a way that those being supported can also teach their supporters some other skill, this grouping will be very effective.

Grouping Type #7:

Diverse Groups

Diverse groups are mixed in terms of sex, ethnicity (where relevant) and achievement levels. This type of grouping is optimal for long term cooperative formats as they maximise potential for peer tutoring, social development and classroom management - whilst avoiding cliques which can lead to bullying, refusal to work, lack of social interaction and other classroom management issues.

It is this particular type of grouping which has been shown through numerous research studies to show significant gains in academic achievement and motivation.

Generally, a diverse group will consist of a high achiever, a low achiever and two middle achievers, and it will consist of males and females. When appropriate, ethnic groups will also be equally represented. Forming and managing these groupings is obviously not as straightforward as random groupings.

Diverse groups are created for long term projects (usually spanning three to six weeks at least) and we will cover suitable project types in later sections. If groups are changed more frequently than this there is insufficient time for individuals to bond as a team and if they are never changed, the opportunities for students to use their social skills in new groupings are lost.

Groups should be changed from time to time, even when team members are working well together to give students the chance to bond with others in the class and also to give team members a break from each other. Invariably, some teams won't get on as harmoniously as others; subjecting Itchy and Scratchy to the same groupings for a whole half term of work is unfair and will be detrimental to their own development (as well as creating unnecessary management issues).

Although diverse groups have been shown to stimulate academic achievement this method should never be the only grouping type used in cooperative sessions. If it were, the benefits of the other types of groupings would not be realised. From time to time therefore, the teacher should use groupings such as mixed skills, similar skills, interest, performance and support groups to get the most from students and allow them to get the most from each other.

Forming Diverse Groups: I'm going to show you two methods - one 'low tech', and one using a spreadsheet application.

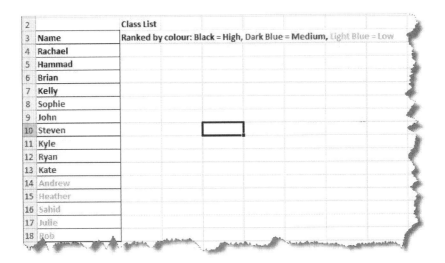

Regardless of the method you use, you will need the following in order to progress: a class list with students ranked according to their ability level. To make it simple, we rank ability by three broad groups – Low, Medium and High. The following picture shows what I mean but it doesn't have to be completed in a spreadsheet. You can use paper, or the back of a beermat if you're doing this in the pub and you've managed to find a dry one.

Low-Tech Diverse Grouping Method: Post-It Notes

This method is very easy to orchestrate and provides a really easy way of changing groups around if they're not working. It also provides a handy visual reference for students.

Using your ability-ranked class list write the name of each student on a colour-coded post-it note. Remember that the medium ability students will be sub-divided into two groups so that you will have four groups in total – mediums on one colour note, highs on another and the two low groups each on two different coloured notes.

Groups can now be selected by taking one student from each colour group and putting them together on a team sheet (a large piece of paper or card). Individuals can easily be moved from group to group until a satisfactory grouping is obtained, thanks to the wonderful restickable properties of the post-it note, and the finished team sheet can then be put on display for easy reference. Remember that some students just love to mess teachers around by changing the arrangement of the notes to cause confusion. You can prevent that by coating the sheet with some clear polythene, or by employing the traditional method of shouting at them.

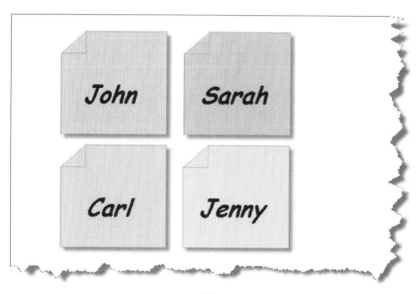

A note on gender: Of course it may not always be possible to have an equal ratio of boys to girls on each team - but wherever possible do try to avoid having one boy with three girls, or vice versa. This grouping usually results in the odd one out either being totally ignored or, if the gene pool has been kind to them, being given undue attention. It is better to have two of each sex on as many teams as possible and then, if necessary, have a team all of the same sex for the remainders. If you would like a way to effortlessly create Diverse Learning Teams, I have included a piece of software for you with this book called **Team Maker**™. It is in your online resources section.

Managing group work sessions

Obviously, you can't just put students into groups and expect the session to run smoothly – it takes careful management and well-planned organised activities to run a successful session of group work.

This section concerns management of group work sessions so that problems are, as much as is possible, prevented from happening. The more effectively you pre-empt and prevent problems, the more pleasant and manageable the session will be.

The first step in preventing problems is to make sure all students know exactly what they will be doing during the session. In our classroom management courses we use the analogy of giving them a clear map to follow – "Give them a clear map to follow and there is more chance of them getting where you want them to go."

This means giving very clear, step by step instructions which prevent misinterpretation as far as possible. Steer clear from words such as 'appropriately', 'properly' and 'quietly', which are abstract terms and mean different things to different individuals. When our instructions are open to misinterpretation we open the door to arguments...

Teacher: *"Work quietly"*

Student: *"I am working quietly!"*

See what I mean? Unless we stipulate exactly what is meant by the word 'quietly', we are going to get students working at different noise levels and each of them can then, quite legitimately, argue that they are working quietly.

Definite phrases and **precise instructions** leave no room for such arguments.

A **definite phrase,** for example, could be "Work in silence". There is no argument with this since there are no degrees of silence: you're either being silent or you're not. A student can't say "I was being silent" if they were making a noise.

If that's too draconian for you, use **precise instructions** instead. A precise instruction could be "Work at noise level two" (assuming you are displaying a noise level meter in the room) or "Use your 'Partner Voices'" (having first explained to students what you mean by 'partner voices' together with the acceptable noise level when using them).

Here's another simple example of how precise instructions cut out arguments. Which set of instructions is likely to get the desired result?

A) Teacher: *"Get on with your work please."*

B) Teacher: *"Ryan, you need to finish drawing the diagram and get it labeled in the next ten minutes. After that, answer questions 1-4 underneath your diagram. OK? Now tell me what I just asked you to do please."*

Can you see how Teacher B asks Ryan to repeat her instructions? This cuts out the need for Ryan to say "I didn't understand what you wanted me to do" or "I didn't hear you" - one less problem to deal with.

Use precise instructions to explain to students the objectives of the task, the procedure to complete it and materials to use.

The second step in preventing problems in group work sessions (or any classroom activity for that matter) is to teach the behaviour that you want to see.

When I run coaching and training sessions at schools I'm amazed at the number of teachers who wait for something to go wrong in the classroom before doing anything about it. This is backward. Instead of waiting for students to get it wrong, why not SHOW (ie 'teach') them what you want them to do in advance so that they have as much chance as possible of getting it right?

If you have a student who continually fails to hand homework in when it is due, is there any point in continually waiting for them to do so and then punishing them when they don't? There is a reason why the homework isn't being done and if we can address the reason there is perhaps more chance that the task will be completed in future.

We can't always address the reasons for behaviour – many are outside our control but sometimes the extra support shown to a student who is facing outside pressures is enough to encourage them to make positive changes. A better way, for example, than continual punishment to deal with a student who 'forgets' to do their homework would be to 'teach' them some time-management skills.

There are three main ways to teach your students how you want them to behave during group work...

1. Establish routines

2. Explain & model desired actions

3. Assign student roles

1. Establishing Routines

I'm often asked by teachers how they can become more consistent and the best way I've found to create instant consistency is the humble routine. A routine cements your instructions in place so that they are the same every time. This means your students develop the right habits through repetition. It is when we give different instructions for a task that we get inconsistencies – and it is difficult for a student to know what to do when the rules or instructions keep changing.

For group work, you need to think about what you want your students to do and how you want them to behave during the group work session.

Think about 'hot spot' and problem areas - issues which always tend to create problems, such as asking for help or wandering round the room aimlessly bumping into things. These problems need to be pre-empted and prevented by being written into your routine – as in the following example.

Sample Routine for Group Work

- **Stay in your allotted group**

- **Ask your team members for help if you have a questions**

- **Help your team mates if you are asked for help**

- **Ask for help from the teacher only when the group agrees on the same question**

- **Work within stated noise levels**

Once you've decided on a routine it needs to be taught to students, the same way you would introduce and teach any new topic. Demonstrate what you want students to do at each stage of the routine and exactly how you want them to act. Then have them practice this several times over the next few sessions until the routine becomes a habit. Have the routine laminated and displayed on the wall for reference.

You will probably find there are steps within the routine which could become routines in themselves - such as the steps to take to 'ask for help' in the correct manner. If you want your students to ask for help in a certain way, they need to be shown or taught the specific way – with another routine.

Routines really can automate your classroom and any change to your normal teaching can be made much easier for everyone by turning it into a routine.

2. Explaining & Modelling Acceptable Behaviour

Group work is the perfect medium for reinforcing social skills – in any group work session students naturally have to interact with each other. In order to cut out problems and ensure they interact in an acceptable manner, key social skills need to be explained and modelled prior to the session. Remember – it's all about giving them a clear map to follow.

The following social skills should be demonstrated/explained prior to, and continually modelled during group work sessions.

• **Listening skills** – explain how you want students to listen to each other.

• **Remaining calm when others do something you don't agree with/coping with conflict** – group work naturally promotes discussions which can become heated at times. Students therefore need to be shown how to keep their tempers and remain calm (we'll assume you have frisked them for weapons before class).

• **Helping when someone is struggling & encouraging team spirit** – learning to act as a team player is something which doesn't come naturally to some students. It needs to be explained and taught, before and during the session.

3. Assigning roles

The reason some students do nothing during group work and others lazily copy from other students is that they do not have specific tasks or jobs to complete during the session. By assigning student roles you give accountability – students are involved from the start of the task.

For instance, in a group of four:

Student 1 could be responsible for materials - collecting the materials/resources and returning them to the appropriate place when the day or period is over; making sure none get lost (materials, not students) and that damages are reported to the teacher.

Student 2 could be responsible for seeing that the steps of the activity are followed.

Student 3 could be responsible for making observations, recording data, and taking minutes as the activity progresses.

Student 4 could be responsible for overseeing the writing of the group report.

Other roles might include:

Quality controller – checks other students' work and corrects mistakes.

Mr/Mrs Motivator - encourages team members to participate when enthusiasm is waning.

Presenter - feeds back to the rest of the class by way of individual or group presentation.

Assigning roles can be undertaken by the teacher or the students themselves but where pupil strengths and weaknesses are particularly pronounced, the teacher should be the one doing it.

What to do when some students won't do their share of the work in a group

This is a common problem, particularly with diverse/mixed ability groups - but your first response should NOT be to jump in and solve the problem. Whenever possible, your students should be given the opportunity to solve these problems themselves and develop social skills.

Solving conflicts proactively and appropriately is a very valuable skill for team members to learn. Your role is to be on hand and help the group if they struggle to solve the problem themselves.

• Talk to other members of the group and encourage them to help each other.

• Encourage group members to offer support to the pupil who isn't working and make sure he/she fully understands what they are expected to do.

• Encourage group members to suggest an achievable work target for their team mate.

If the student is still refusing to work:

• Take them aside and explain that they may have to be taken off group work if they can't stick to the rules.

• Withdraw the pupil and give them individual work to do.

• Laminate them and mount them on the wall.

• Show them any episode of 'The A-Team' (last resort!)

Sample Cooperative Learning Activity:

Peer Lessons

Overview: There is some truth in the old saying 'You never really learn a subject until you teach it'. In this activity, each group is involved in preparing and teaching new information to the rest of the class.

Number of people: Any group size.

Materials: Suitable teaching and resource preparation materials should be made available for students to choose from including poster making materials, visual aids and props.

Time: This activity is designed to last for an entire lesson although additional time (during preceding lessons) needs to be allocated for preparation and research.

Directions:

1. Students are placed in teams of four. Teams can be randomly selected but this activity works best with diverse groupings so that low ability students can be given the motivation and support they may need.

2. Each group is given a topic, skill, concept or piece of information to teach to the rest of the group.

3. Students are given time to research their task and decide how they will present their information (in a preceding lesson). They are encouraged to avoid lecture presentations so as to make the learning experience as active as possible and must make sure all group-members are involved in some capacity in the teaching process.

Suggestions for teaching methods could include:

• Visual aids

• Role-plays/skits

• Quiz games and puzzles

• Q and A sessions

• Puzzles

• Practical sessions

• Production of worksheets, handouts and reading material

4. Each group presents their lesson to the rest of the class For further information on managing group work sessions as well as a huge range of ready-made cooperative & active learning lesson formats and activities, see my book 'The Active Learning Tool Kit' It's available on Amazon.

COMMUNICATE With Your Students

If you think about it, all relationships have communication at their heart. You can't have a relationship of any kind unless communication is involved in some form so it's not surprising we have poor relationships with our most challenging students – they're usually among the last people we 'chat along nicely' with.

Getting them to open up and start communicating with you is the first hurdle. Striking up a conversation with your average, maladjusted 14 year old is difficult – especially when you don't know them very well.

It's a vicious circle; you can't get to know them until you have something to talk about and you have little to talk about with them until you get to know them better. The problem is having something to talk about. We need a 'way-in' and that's exactly what I'm going to give you...

'Way-in' #1: Ask them for advice

When people are given the chance to express their opinions it shows that you value them and what they have to say. It's empowering – people like to feel important and valued. Ask your students questions that allow them to express their interests and ideas - things they know about. Girls love to give advice on fashion, hair styles, make up, jewellery etc and tend to be experts on soaps on TV. Boys like to give advice on computer games, sports and pretty much anything practical. So if you're stuck for something to say to your students start by asking their advice. You might ask some of the girls for their opinion on what you should wear for an upcoming party or suggesting a suitable CD for your own child's birthday. You might ask for a run-down of the latest happenings on the current hot soap or ask them a decent shop to buy a new bag for you or your spouse. If you're trying to strike up a conversation with a boy try getting him to help you with something of a practical nature. I once took my mountain bike into school with me and asked three of my new students to help me fit some parts at lunch time. Prior to this day I had really struggled to break the ice with these boys but we never looked back after our 'cycle workshop' session – it was a great way to start a conversation and start building a relationship with them.

Tip: When it comes to talking about personal matters make sure it is their advice you're asking for – not their opinion. Asking a student what they think of your new hairstyle may set you up for ridicule while asking them to suggest a decent hairdresser probably won't.

'Way-in' #2: Ask a favour

When we think about ways to build bonds with people we intuitively think along the lines of doing something good for them or trying to be more like them. Suggestions include things like mirroring their body language, matching facial expressions, offering to help them etc. The 18th century politician and extreme kite-flyer Benjamin Franklin found an alternative, counter-intuitive approach which was equally, if not more, effective: asking favours.

To cut a long story very short, he had apparently been trying to connect with a fellow politician but just wasn't able to; the other man wanted nothing at all to do with him. Franklin knew that this man happened to have a certain rare book in his personal library and he asked if he could borrow it from him. Surprisingly, the man's attitude towards Franklin changed completely from that moment on...

"When we next met in the House, he spoke to me (which he had never done before), and with great civility; and he ever after manifested a readiness to serve me on all occasions."

Franklin attributed this to a simple principle –

- if you want to increase the likelihood of someone liking you, get them to do you a favour.

It does make sense – when you help someone out or do something positive for them you naturally feel a connection with them; contribution feels good, there is joy in giving.

So, next time you're trying to make a connection and find a way in with a student, remember the **Franklin Effect**. You could ask them to help you sort a problem with your laptop, carry some heavy equipment, help design a wall display, decorate your house; perhaps even do your ironing.

'Way-in' #3: Share some of your life

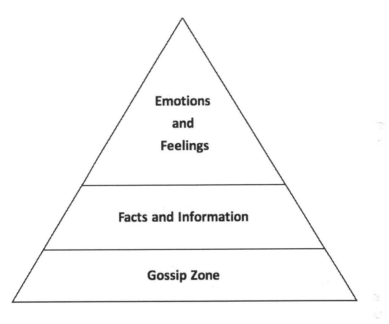

The pyramid above shows different levels of communication. The most basic level is the 'Gossip Zone'. This is the area of playground chatter and banter. Conversations about football scores, latest soap happenings, the injustices of the X Factor panel, and most of the discussions in the House of Commons, take place at this level.

At the second level we talk about facts and we give out information. Most teacher-talk in the classroom takes place on this level.

Finally, we have the top level at which emotions and feelings are discussed. When conversations take place at this level there is more risk for those taking part – more of the self is revealed. Leaders who communicate on this level truly inspire their listeners because they reach them on a deep level; they connect with them.

Relationships with your students can develop very quickly when communication involves feelings and emotions, and when you start sharing some aspects of your life with them. Laugh and joke with them frequently and if you're down, explain why – let them see that you're human and it will encourage them to do the same.

Way-in #4: Use WRITTEN communication

Don't underestimate this – it can be a very powerful way of connecting with some students – particularly those who are reluctant to talk face to face. There are all kinds of ways of using the written word to build relationships. Here are a few you could try:

Notes:

Notes can be hand-written or typed. Always start with something positive before mentioning your concerns as shown in these two examples:

Example of a note to a late/tardy student:

Dear...

It was wonderful to see you in class today; the lesson always has a lively atmosphere when you're around. 😊 For that reason it would be nice to see more of you! Can you make sure you're in class ON TIME tomorrow please so that I don't get worried about you? Remember, lessons start at 9:10am sharp so you really to be outside my room by 9:05am.

See you in the morning...

Example of a note to a student who forgets to hand in homework:

Dear...

The work you did in class today was very good – well done. It's so nice to see you putting in more effort and you really can do well when you try can't you? Come to think of it, you could do even better if you would get your homework in on time. Just in case you didn't write it down, tonight's homework is on the class blog here (link)...

If you need any help on it make sure you catch me before going home tonight so we can make sure you do a good job on it. Let's make it 'Your Best Ever Homework'.

I'll look forward to seeing you on Wednesday when you hand it in to me.

Cards:

• **Birthday cards:** Go a step further than saying 'Happy Birthday'. Make them feel special by sending a card (posting it home gets bonus points).

• **'Thank You' cards:** When they do something right/good, saying 'thank you' shows you've noticed and are grateful. Giving them a card in an envelope says much more.

• **'Get Well' cards:** Go a step further than marking them absent on the register – send a card.

Post-It Notes:

Marking books is a great chance to build relationships because the comments often develop into private conversations. By using post-it notes or even writing directly in their books you can ask them questions, send them good wishes, congratulate them on an achievement, tell them jokes and give feedback of all kinds. These private little dialogues all go towards conveying the message that you care about and value them.

Way-in #5: Give sincere compliments

We all respond to compliments but while this is a sure-fire way to connect with a student and get them listening to you it really will only work if your comments are genuine. Kids are great at reading our true feelings and sugar-coated flattery will harm a relationship rather than build it.

It is hard sometimes finding things about which to compliment students beyond the classic 'well done' and 'that's really good' and yet this strategy is so powerful that it can't be used as an excuse not to do it. One method we have found useful on live courses is to get participants to create their own bank of suitable comment starters like this:

1. "I find it really helpful when you..."

2. "There are some days when someone does something which totally surprises me..."

3. "I know you struggle with... but what you have done there is superb."

4. "What are you like at accepting compliments? I know it can go to people's heads but I've got to say this..."

5. "Okay stop please, everyone, I need to say this. There are three people who deserve special mention for..."

6. "I just want you to know that when you put effort in like that it makes my job worthwhile."

7. I know this hasn't been easy for you so I want you to know I'm doubly impressed about..."

Way-in #6: Do your research – find out their interests

People enjoy talking about things they're actually interested in and young people get a kick out of talking about their hobbies, passions and interests. Clearly, once you know their passions you can easily strike up conversation with them - you have a subject to chat about which will interest and engage them. For example, if their favourite subject turns out to be 'mountain biking' you could:

• Ask their advice about new bikes or related equipment (we all like to be able to show how knowledgeable we are about a subject, particularly if it's our favourite one.

• Bring an old bike into school and ask them to help you fix it.

• Share stories you've seen on TV about mountain biking.

• Make up a list of websites on mountain biking - "Here Jonny, you said you were into mountain biking, I found these websites you might like to look at..."

• Find old books/magazines or newspaper clippings and offer them as a something to look at in their spare time.

• Get them to tell you all about their riding adventures. Perhaps they compete – what a great thing to get them talking about!

The problem, of course, is finding out what their hobbies and interests are in the first place. So how do we discover these? We could just ask them but as we know already, place - they may not be too keen to open up if we have no relationship in place to start with. We need a less invasive way of discovering their interests. Here are six ideas for starters:

'Get to know them' method #1: Questions on the board

Try putting a simple question on the board at the end of the lesson: "What are your three favourite hobbies?", "If you had £20/$20 to spend which shop would you go in and what would you buy?", "What do you do on a Saturday?" etc. Ask students to write their answers on a piece of paper with their name on and leave it in the box by the door on their way out.

'Get to know them' method #2: Questionnaire

I explain these in my main classroom management book – Take Control of the Noisy Class - but you can get a sample editable questionnaire to use as a starting point in your online resource area

These questionnaires are a nice, non-invasive, under-the-radar way to uncover the hobbies, passions and interests of your students and once you do so your ability to start a conversation with them is virtually guaranteed. Everybody likes talking about their favourite subject.

'Get to know them' method #3: Thumb Ball®

The Thumb Ball® is an interactive way to get students talking. Use it as a starter, energiser, getting-to-know-you or Circle Time activity to stimulate peer relationships and discover student interests.

The basic principle is to throw the ball to a member of the group and get them to respond to one of the categories under their thumb when they catch it – hence the name.

The ball is covered in categories relating to a central theme such as 'skills', 'hobbies' or 'personal qualities' and can easily be adapted to fit virtually any curriculum area. You can make your own thumb ball by writing categories on a sponge ball or you can buy one from www.thumball.com.

'Get to know them' method #4: Suggestion Box

Have a cardboard box on your desk and invite students at the end of a session to give you some information about their interests. "On your way out please write your favourite hobby/team/band/sport etc on a piece of paper with your name on and leave it in the box on my desk."

'Get to know them' method #5: Computer Time

Give students ten minutes of free time on the internet and monitor which sites they visit. (It is obviously assumed that measures are in place to prevent them from visiting sites they 'really' want to visit!

Making time to talk with your students

A huge challenge for most teachers is finding the time to do all this relationship building stuff. Many secondary teachers teach several hundred different students every day and feel that getting to know them all would be an almost impossible task and one probably more trouble than it's worth. Indeed, one of the most common objections which crops up when we talk about this subject on live courses is...

"I'm a busy teacher, how am I supposed to find the time to build relationships with challenging students?"

I suppose we first need to think about the amount of time you currently spend mopping up incidents and dealing with students who don't work or follow instructions. How much time does that currently waste? Many teachers complain that they are unable to do their jobs purely because of the time spent dealing with behaviour problems. Students are more likely to behave for a teacher they respect, trust and get on with so spending time building relationships with them is going to save you time in the long run.

Here are four simple ways of making time to build relationships:

1. Delegate administration tasks

This method kills two birds with one stone – our most challenging students are usually crying out for attention and would almost certainly benefit from being given a responsibility of some kind. By delegating administration tasks – such as taking the register, collecting lunch money, photocopying, preparing equipment etc. we meet this need and also free ourselves up with some time to spend with other students.

2. Break times/lunch times

One of my colleagues who teaches full time spends every break time with students. His door is always open, he has board games set up and students know they can drop in for a quiet chat, help with problems or just a bit of fun. He rarely has problems with behaviour in his lessons because students respect the fact that he is there for them and wants to help them.

3. Yard Duty/Bus Duty

Another colleague actually enjoys yard duty and bus duty – she says she finds the students respect the fact that she is going out of her way to spend time with them. I often hear from teachers who make a point of eating their lunch with students – chatting over a meal is relaxing, and students tend to open up more when they are relaxed.

4. Before lessons

Outside your classroom before the lesson is a great opportunity to get talking to your students. These first few moments are important in setting a pleasant and friendly tone and making them feel welcome in your classroom. Spending a few moments interacting and chatting informally with them makes you more approachable and can work wonders in settling students before the lesson starts.

Also remember, you don't need to focus your efforts on EVERY student you teach. That would take a lot of time. The students who cause problems are the ones to focus your efforts on – they are the ones who will benefit from the extra support and attention, the ones who suffer from the de-motivators we talked about in the introduction. Obviously this doesn't mean ignoring the other students – it just means making sure those who really need to feel valued and appreciated by an adult do so.

This brings us nicely on to...

Belonging Strategy # 3:

The Relationship Challenge

On my live courses I like to introduce an activity called the 'Relationship Challenge'. Briefly, this involves making a definite commitment to improve relationships with any particularly hard to reach students who are causing you difficulties.

The idea is that you totally focus on improving your relationship with just one student at a time. That's not to say you ignore the others, but that you make more of an effort with this one student. The reason should be obvious. Without focus the days, weeks and months pass by quickly and you may well find yourself getting to the end of the school year not having truly connected with this, or any, student. Missing all the benefits associated with positive relationships would be a terrible waste of time and a lost opportunity to make life easier for both of you.

So, the idea is to aim to spend just ONE MINUTE a day for twenty days (four working weeks) engaged in relationship-building conversation with this particular student – and then see how your relationship with them changes. If you find yourself doing more, even better; the target is just one minute, more than that is a bonus. Everyone can manage one minute.

Just to clarify, 'relationship-building conversation' doesn't mean ordering them to sit properly in lessons or asking them why their homework hasn't been handed in; it's in addition to normal, day to day, instructional conversation. You can talk about anything at all – TV, music, class work/their favourite topics, football scores, asking them where they bought their cool new shoes, anything including their hobbies and interests (which you've discovered using the methods above, of course).

One minute isn't a huge amount of time by anyone's standards but of course it is going to take more than a 'Hi, how's it going?' to fill it. On the days that you teach the student you will easily manage it during the lesson while other students are working but on other days you will need to be more creative. It may mean actively seeking the student out in the lunch or bus queue; scheduling a weekly, private 'how can I help you more with your work?' meeting; having lunch with them; or just catching them in the corridor or outside your room before/after the lesson. There are countless opportunities to connect with students through the simple art of conversation – it is just a matter of taking advantage of them.

I receive emails all the time from teachers who have tried this method telling us about the wonderful effect it has had on their teaching and their students. There is, however, one very important thing to keep in mind...

WARNING:

Initially you will almost certainly encounter reluctance and negativity, and in some circumstances all this extra attention can actually 'freak out' some students. All the strategies we've mentioned are powerful relationship builders but if you go in too hard, too heavy and too fast, you can find students running in the opposite direction.

We've all played the 'Attraction-Rejection' game (the more attention we give to someone, the more they back away) so the trick is to tread carefully at first. If you go running up to a student with whom you've never connected and suddenly offer them a pile of magazines ("Here I got you these because I know you're interested in mountain biking!") and hit them with a load of personal probing questions out of the blue they are going to wonder, naturally, what on earth is going on.

At best they'll ignore you. At worst (particularly if you press too hard) they'll think you're 'weird' and all efforts to build a relationship from that point on will have a new obstacle – suspicion. Go easy, take it slowly; relationships take time to build – particularly with very challenging students.

That said, here are two ways with which you can't really go wrong:

1. Give sincere compliments (see **'Way-Ins'** above),

2. Offering support – particularly where work is concerned.

I remember one young 15 year old lad in a class I was covering whose behaviour truly pushed the envelope of unmanageability. The first lesson I had with him was a battle from bell to bell – he just would not settle, would not engage and was intent on wrecking the entire lesson.

I caught him next lesson at the door and asked him to wait with me while the other students went in. He thought he was going to get a rollicking for last lesson's performance and was rather taken aback when I said:

"You know what Jake? Last lesson I couldn't help feeling there was something wrong; you didn't seem happy at all. I don't want you coming to my lessons and having a bad time, I don't want to be on your case having a go at you." I smiled at him and he looked up at me as I continued. *"My lessons are supposed to be useful to you, I want you to get something out of them. Can you tell me what I can do to make it better for you please?"*

There was a long pause as he tried to make sense of what I was saying. Then he opened up, as if I'd turned a tap on. He began to tell me how he couldn't see the board, how he couldn't read very well and was supposed to wear glasses, how other students made fun of him if he did, and how he didn't understand most of what was going on. His behaviour was the classic result of the de-motivators we talked about in the introduction.

We had to cut our conversation short so that I could get in to start the lesson but those few moments outside the classroom were the beginning of a very different relationship between Jake and me.

He now saw me as someone who was there to help him and I saw him as a young boy who needed help. I made a few changes to accommodate his weaknesses and gave him some extra support and his behavior miraculously changed overnight. He arrived to lessons with a smile and his hand shot up almost every time I asked a question. The effort he now put into his work was *unbelievable.*

Assignment 2

1) Schedule student meetings: Arrange a meeting for small groups of your most challenging students

Pick groups of four to five students who have low motivation and explain to them you need their help in improving the lessons for them. Pick a time which they won't find inconvenient (eg five or ten minutes before the end of the lesson out of earshot of the rest of the group is an option if you can't see them returning during break time). Depending on the size and needs of the group you could schedule multiple meetings – one in each lesson.

2) Talk & Connect: Make a point of talking/chatting with your most challenging students

Use the Relationship Challenge and any of the ideas in Belonging Strategy #2 to start to connect and build bonds with your challenging students.

3) Include Team-building activities in lessons: Research and plan to include regular team-building activities with your group

Team-building activities as described above can be integrated into lessons as a starter, fill-in or as a curriculum learning aid.

Aim to include at least one 'fun' team-building activity per fortnight with a difficult, unmotivated group.

Start a file or folder of suitable team-building activities and start to include them in your lessons from now.

4) Include Group Work in Lessons: Research and set up Cooperative Learning Activities

It is beyond the scope of this program to provide activities for Cooperative Group work – suitability will depend on the particular group and the work/lesson topic being covered. We have, however, included comprehensive information on forming groups and managing group work – sufficient to get started. Suitable cooperative learning activities can be found online or in my book on this subject, '**The Active Learning Tool Kit**'. It is available on Amazon.

Ideally, all your lessons should have a cooperative learning element built in so that students collaborate and work together. As a minimum, aim to set up <u>at least </u>one active/cooperative learning session per week.

Start a file or folder of suitable activities and start to include them in your lessons from now.

4) Get them involved in changing the classroom environment: Ask individuals and/or groups of students to be responsible for certain aspects of the classroom environment

Ask selected students to take responsibility for any of the ideas in 'Community Builder #2' above.

Enjoying this book so far? I'd love it for you to share your thoughts and post a quick review on Amazon!

Just head over to Amazon, search for the book title and click on the 'Write a customer review' button!

Strategies to Satisfy the Need for Power

Power Strategy #1:

Give them responsibility

The students who present most problems in class – those who command attention of staff and peers because of their dominant personalities will continue to demand attention until they get it. The thing is, these students tend to be the 'ring leaders' and often have strong personalities and leadership potential. One of the best ways to give these students the attention they crave without spending the whole lesson running round after them is by giving them some responsibilities.

A power-oriented student given the responsibility of being in control becomes less of a problem. Giving these students responsibility sends a message that you trust them, and does as much to cement positive relationships as it does to empower them.

Responsibility can take many forms: being in charge of certain equipment; monitoring and supporting more vulnerable members of the class (such as victims of bullying); allowing students the opportunity to grade their own work; letting them choose lesson activities.

Here are some ways to give tough students an element of control through responsibility:

• **Set up Buddy Schemes.** Buddy Schemes can be set up on a school-wide or class-wide basis and the results they bring are often amazing. The basic premise is simple (one student helps another) but the benefits are deep and powerful (for both students), and they can bring about quite miraculous changes in the most challenging students.

Example: There is truth in the belief that the best way to learn something is to teach it to someone else. A buddy scheme can be set up in which the student, rather than receiving the usual punishment for a transgression, is given a 'buddy' to look after, tutor or assist. The buddy can be a younger student or one in the same year group of lower ability, or perhaps with special educational needs. Suitable responsibilities might include providing support – eg if the student is a victim of bullying, helping with academic tasks such as reading, tutoring in sport or running a break time or lunch time activity. The potential of this should not be underestimated – on more than one occasion I have seen tough, very hard-to-reach students dramatically try to change themselves into positive role models when given the task of mentoring another student.

- **Give them responsibility for <u>teaching</u> the lesson.** Giving control of the lesson to a student and letting them 'teach' the lesson can be enlightening for both student and teacher. Not surprisingly, students who take this opportunity tend to learn a tremendous amount from the experience, not least respect for you, once they see how challenging teaching can be!

Example: Give an unmotivated student the opportunity to teach part of the lesson in any way they choose and in a way they feel will encourage their peers to listen and take part. Allow them to work in a pair or small group if they prefer, and provide an optional lesson structure or framework for them.

This method can be introduced to students by telling them you need their help as you are struggling to get their attention. (See 'Ask a Favour' Way-in 2, Belonging Strategy #2). Tell them what is coming up in future lessons and give them a choice of topic to teach. Then set up a timetable with them so to help them plan their lesson. Make sure you give them a 'get out of jail free' card by adding that you will teach the lesson for them if they decide they can't manage it for whatever reason – impress upon them though that in return you would expect their cooperation and attention.

• **Give them responsibility for <u>managing</u> the lesson.** If you have students who are not responding to your instructions (despite threats and punishments) it could be because they feel a perceived lack of power. Give them responsibility (and therefore power) by letting them ensure rules and procedures are followed by other students. This often works wonders and, as with the above method, can be enlightening for the students themselves by enabling them to empathise with the teacher and the difficulties they face when trying to manage challenging behaviour in the classroom.

Example: Speak with selected students and get them to identify problem behaviours which are impeding learning in their class. Offer them the opportunity to manage these problems by giving simple reminders and directions to students so that the lesson can run without interruption. Give them instruction in the best way to direct students without creating conflict, and discuss suitable consequences which can also be administered when necessary.

• **Give them responsibility for the activities & tasks in a lesson.** By giving students an element of control over the particular activities they can choose in a lesson, they have less need to derive power by opting out and arguing about the limited choices on offer. There are fewer power struggles when students are given choices about expected outcomes.

Example: If the aim of a lesson is to explain the key points about a given process, does it matter how that aim is met? Instead of dictating that they complete a single designated task, try giving them a limited choice in the form of a voting slip (a verbal discussion can sometimes lead to arguments and a vote is more fun).

"Which of the following tasks would you prefer?"

a) Produce a mind-map on........

b) Produce a newspaper report on.......

c) Work as a group to find a solution to......

d) Complete exercise.........

The activity with the most votes wins and by taking part in this vote you agree to take part in the chosen activity without argument."

• **Give them a job.** Jobs for students might include: set up or take down equipment; safety monitors; noise level monitors; group motivators; liaison with hard to reach students; errand runners; photocopying; arranging wall displays; collecting trip money etc. One of the most successful roles we've seen implemented at a school is the VIP.

Example: The job of a VIP is to welcome new students and visitors and act as first port of call for other students who are experiencing problems of any kind. VIPs also have special privileges such as break time refreshments, computer time etc. The role can be awarded on a rotation basis or as a spontaneous reward for good effort. At one primary school I was working in recently the VIPs were given Day-Glo workmen's waistcoats to wear as a uniform so they could be easily identified.

Some teachers feel uncomfortable giving responsibilities and special jobs to a student who normally causes problems: "It's not fair on the students who behave well".

It's a fair point - but we have to remember that all students have different needs. Your students are aware of this, they know that Jonny tends to get more attention from the teacher because he needs it; they know that he needs differentiated work and special arrangements put in place to help him cope with his special needs. In most cases students are happy to see other students being catered for – especially if it means they can get on with their own work without being interrupted. But what about those students who do take offence? Sometimes we may need to explain why Jonny is being given special jobs to do and the analogy of a car mechanic usually works quite well:

A mechanic can't use the same tool for every problem when a car breaks down – different problems require different tools. If he tried to use the same tool to fix a broken head gasket as he did to change the oil, he wouldn't get very far (nor would the car once he'd finished with it). In the same way that the mechanic needs to assess a problem and then pick the right tool to deal with it, the teacher has to choose appropriate strategies to deal with a wide range of individual student problems.

Power Strategy #2:

Give them opportunity to achieve and succeed

Achievement brings a feeling of personal satisfaction and accomplishment - and the real internal motivation that results is reward itself. If a person feels satisfied that they have reached a level of success or feels good about what they have accomplished, there is no need for external reward. The joy of achievement is a great feeling, and one of our most powerful motivators, because it is linked to survival – if you're no good, you lose out. Students welcome opportunities to feel competent, to achieve and succeed.

Remember, one of the reasons for a lack of student motivation is **fear of failure and embarrassment.** By addressing their lack of knowledge and giving clear, scaffolded instruction we can bypass this hurdle whilst meeting a very powerful need – the need to achieve and feel successful.

Achievement is met by providing interesting work at the right level of challenge and by giving just enough guidance & support to enable them to succeed without having the work done for them.

Here's a five-point plan to ensure your lessons give students maximum chance of experiencing success and achievement...

1. Tell students precisely what they need to do in order to succeed. Don't let your students struggle to figure out what is expected of them. Reassure students that they can do well in your course, and tell them exactly what they must do to succeed. Under-achieving students may need everything explained in a step-by-step fashion.

Remember also, a good recipe book will not just list instructions in a sequence of orders; it gives some explanation as to why you are being asked to complete each step, eg 'the reason you maintain a low temperature while adding the lemon juice is to prevent the mixture from curdling'. It might also include some pictures to illustrate each step in greater detail. There might be some 'tips' for saving time and avoiding mistakes as well as advice on suitable times to prepare the meal, and perhaps even suggestions as to alternative ingredients. These extra pieces of information give some background to the various stages involved in following the recipe and make it more interesting, enjoyable and purposeful.

Your instructions need to answer students' most pressing questions about a new topic:

• What am I being asked to do?

• How exactly am I supposed to do it?

• When and where will I be able to apply what I've learned? (In other words, what is the point in doing this/what are the benefits to me?)

• How will I know when I'm doing it right?

2. Ensure early success. To be motivated to continue with any new task you must start at the most basic level. I took some lessons in fly fishing many years ago and had to stand in a field in order to master casting without a hook; only after that could I progress to looking slightly less silly by casting from a river bank; and then finally they let me loose with my rod in a small boat. If they'd started me out in the wrong order (in the boat) I would have ended up a very tangled, stressful mess, probably put off fly fishing (a very sedate, relaxing hobby) for life. I learned the right way – though I still haven't caught any flies.

Similarly, when you're learning to drive a car you start off in car parks and open spaces before being allowed into the nightmares that are town centres. Learn a new language and you'll master basic verbs and nouns before they let you loose on whole sentences.

If motivation of students is our goal we have to structure tasks which virtually guarantee early success. Once the simple tasks have been mastered we can move them up a stage and at each stage they gain a sense of achievement and mastery before moving on. Nothing is more important to student motivation than initial success so take care to set initial tasks at an achievable level or ask simple questions before providing progressively more challenging activities.

3. Always reinforce new material. As soon as a new concept or subject has been presented via text reading, teacher instruction, video or discussion, allow the students to put the concept into action immediately by completing a simple consolidation assignment. These assignments can be very short and should preferably include a cooperative learning element such as the one presented below (taken from one of my other books 'The Active Learning Tool Kit').

Ready, Steady, TEACH!

After explaining or demonstrating a new concept to the class have partners teach the main points to each other. It is most helpful to demonstrate EXCELLENT teaching first by making sure each partner understands the importance of CLARITY (sticking to 1-3 main points covered) and ENERGY (speaking with enthusiasm and passion). Peer teaching is a phenomenally powerful method for improving understanding – hence the saying 'you don't actually learn anything until you teach it'.

Keep sessions very brief, either to sum up lesson content, as a review activity or as a reminder to reinforce some difficult new information and always demonstrate and encourage appropriate, positive communication.

e.g.

i) 5 minutes: Partner one teaches; partner two listens.

ii) Partner two thanks partner one and gives appropriate feedback (See below).

iii) 5 minutes: Partner two teaches; partner one listens and gives feedback.

Appropriate feedback:

Thank you, I agree with...

I liked the way you explained...

I think you're very good at...

The best thing you brought up was...

4. Check students' work as early as possible. We improve by learning from our mistakes so that we do not repeat them. For that to happen we need to know when we've done something wrong and know how to put it right – we need to check our work (or have it checked by someone else) and receive further guidance and instruction along the way. This is an essential part of the learning process if we are to experience a feeling of success and achievement.

Students will become frustrated if they are left wasting time, making mistake after mistake. If the first mistakes are corrected a great deal of stress can be avoided, new skills practised, and sense of achievement gained. We must not give too much help, however – when you simply give the solution, you rob students of the chance to think for themselves and to experience success.

During a lesson observation early in my career I delivered what I thought to be an outstanding science lesson to a group of low-ability KS3 children. They were struggling with some of the procedures and equipment (we were investigating insulation) so I made sure each child was given maximum support and guidance. It wasn't until it was pointed out to me in the debrief that I realised what I had done wrong – I had done most of the work for them! How could they learn when I was taking the opportunity away from them?

The key to 'improvement' is to get the students themselves to work out their own solutions and to give them the tools and skills to work independently. If that's to happen they need to know how to improve their own work – how to check it, correct it and learn from the corrections.

When problems do appear in students' work try to get them to identify the specific problem they have encountered. Unless they know exactly where they are going wrong, they are unlikely to work out how to do it right.

How to help students overcome learning hurdles:

i. Pinpoint the problem

Rather than accepting 'Sir, I can't do this', ask them to tell you what it is, exactly, that they don't 'get'. Doing so focuses them on the problem at hand and reduces their anxiety and frustration.

ii. Break the solution into simple steps

Once the specific problem has been identified, ask them to try and build up a solution in gradual steps through further questioning and simplified examples. Ask them to build on what they already do know.

iii. Praise them

As students work through the steps they've identified be quick to acknowledge progress and further encourage them.

If you follow these steps, students will learn that it is acceptable not to have an instant answer. They will also learn to develop greater patience and to work at their own pace; and by working through the problem, students will experience a sense of achievement and confidence that will increase their motivation to learn.

Only when the student has been made aware of the specific problem they must solve, and is still unable to do so, should we take the reins and correct the error for them.

5. Get them to think about their achievements. It's empowering for students to realise that they have done something right. This is not achieved just by acknowledging their efforts but by getting them to stop and think about what they've done. Doing so not only makes them feel a sense of achievement but also increases the likelihood of them repeating the good behaviour because they will know exactly what to do.

The way to do this is simply to ask them <u>how</u> they have achieved a particular success...

"Hey Jonny, you've managed to work independently for the last fifteen minutes. How did you do that? So if I asked you to work independently again what would you do/how would you do it?"

Power Strategy #3:

Help them set achievable goals and targets

If we want our students to be responsible, self-motivated and capable of working independently, we need to encourage them to analyse their current performance and work on their weaknesses. A great way to do this is to teach them to monitor themselves and to set their own achievable goals and targets.

When students take an active role in setting goals for their work they naturally gain a sense of control and feel more responsible for their own lives – and internal motivation is increased. The perfect time to do this is during 'Student meetings' (Belonging Strategy #1) although it is something which can also be implemented as a lesson starter, a registration activity etc.

Before students can set their own goals they first need to be helped to uncover the behaviours and areas they feel they need to improve. Notice the wording there – they are not being told which behaviours they need to improve (that would just be more external control), they are being helped to analyse and assign, for themselves, the input needed to effect positive changes. Only by learning to think for themselves in this way will they become responsible thinkers.

How to help students set goals:

There are three basic sets of questions to use to get students to think about their current performance and to come up with their own sensible targets and goals:

i. Determine (and get them to confirm) that they want a <u>positive</u> outcome:

"What do you want from these lessons?"

"What are you hoping to gain from your time in school?"

* If they don't come up with a positive answer at this stage (or in response to any of the questions which follow) see below: '*What if they respond negatively or don't answer?*'

ii. Get them to think about their current behaviour:

"Is what you are doing going to get you what you want?"

"Will you get where you want to be if you carry on as you are?"

"What might happen if you carry on doing what you're doing? Is that what you want?"

iii. Get them to suggest alternative courses of action

"What could you do instead?"

"What could you do differently?"

"Can you think of something that would help you get what you want?"

"What else?"

iv. Get them to set targets/goals

"When could you start doing these different things/making these changes?"

"Shall we write these ideas down?"

Notice that throughout this process 'why?' questions are avoided. Asking a student 'why?' is confrontational.

The best goals for students are those which are:

a) Short term (challenging kids' work in the 'here and now' – it is difficult for them to project themselves too far in the future).

b) Simple, straightforward and don't require dramatic changes – small steps are best.

c) Specific – giving the student the details of what, when, where and how they will be achieved.

Example: "I will fill in my homework diary on Wednesday night and take my homework home. I will ask my teacher to explain anything I don't understand. I will finish my homework at home before I play on my X-Box and hand it in on Friday."

*What if they respond negatively or don't answer?

These questions can be daunting for some students – especially in 1:1 situations – and can result in a habitual answer developing: 'dunno'. In this case you have to be careful not to pressure them further as they will retreat. Try sitting in silence and waiting, with a warm smile so as to show you are not putting them 'on the spot'. It can seem like an eternity to wait for an answer in these circumstances but if you remain silent they will usually open up. Pressing them can zip their mouths shut or worse, provoke anger. I like the analogy of the fizzy bottle that must be opened gently otherwise it erupts – take a step back, take the pressure off them by sitting in silence, but maintain eye contact with a smile.

Power Strategy #4:

Recognise their efforts

I'm sure you've been told a million times that one of the most powerful yet easy-to-apply strategies a teacher can use to instil internal motivation is to give positive recognition for effort and achievements. After all, everyone likes to feel appreciated and to have their efforts acknowledged – if they didn't, all those sweatshop factories making gold plastic trophies would fold overnight.

There is much controversy over the use of praise in schools, however. Some people believe we praise students too often and that excessive use can actually have a demotivating effect. The 'anti-praise' lobby believes students can become dependent on the appreciation of adults and that praise therefore does little to develop confidence in their own abilities - so diminishing internal motivation. Excessive praise, they say, will increase a student's apprehension in the face of new tasks; anxiety that they may not meet the teacher's expectations ("Is my picture alright Miss Smith? Have I done this bit right Miss Smith?"); and ultimately disappointment if they fail and consequently receive less praise than they were hoping for.

Some hold the belief that when students are praised specifically for their intelligence ("you are so clever, you're very bright"), they can become very concerned about their performance in comparison to other students. Students lavishly praised in this way tend to opt for less challenging tasks, perhaps in fear of not succeeding, and instead opt for tasks in which they know they will succeed - and for which, therefore, they will receive more praise. Students need to have confidence in their abilities if they are to be motivated, so over-praise is clearly an important factor to be taken into consideration.

There is another potential problem with praise - very often, little concern is given to the driving factors which may lie beneath a students' behaviour. It is entirely possible – for instance, in a classroom environment in which praise is being lavishly strewn about –

to give praise when it is not due, or to reward behaviour prompted by ulterior motives.

Consider this example:

Let's say Jonny (known for dramatic outbursts when provoked by classmates) is sitting quietly in class, and Big George is needling him with unsavoury comments about his mum. On this occasion Jonny displays remarkable self control and manages to ignore Big George – partly because he is helped by Peter and Paul who both jump to his aid with positive comments: "Just ignore him Jonny, he's just trying to wind you up".

Because mature behaviour like this needs to be acknowledged the teacher praises Peter and Paul for being so considerate and helping to avert what would normally have resulted in a messy scuffle between Jonny and George. However (and here's the rub):

Peter was acting out of genuine concern for his friend Jonny's welfare; he simply didn't want to see him get into trouble. Paul, on the other hand, was deliberately manipulating the teacher; he had been in trouble all week himself and came to Jonny's aid purely to get in the teacher's good books.

In this example, both Paul and Peter have received positive recognition from the teacher and, if the psychological belief that 'behaviour which is positively reinforced is more likely to be repeated' is true, then Peter will repeat caring, considerate behaviour and Paul will become increasingly manipulative.

Phew, that's quite an argument against the use of praise, isn't it? Does all this mean that we shouldn't praise students? Is praise really counter-productive in terms of motivation?

Definitely not! But this example highlights potential problems to consider, and shows how the onus is on the teacher - it does mean we have to 'get it right'. Here are some tips to help you navigate this particular minefield:

Making praise more effective:

i. Praise effort rather than achievement

Praise students for their effort alone if they have shown more interest in the challenge of a task and seem more focused on the taking part, rather than the outcome of it and how their results might compare to those of other students. "You've tried so hard, you've really showed determination there".

By focusing on effort rather than achievement we can praise a student even if they fail - and that's very important. Waiting for a child to complete a task before praising them means missing out on untold opportunities to encourage them along the way. If a friend was dieting you wouldn't wait until they had reached their target weight before making positive comments, would you? You'd help them along the way with encouragement, because acknowledging their effort helps them stick in and persevere and, importantly, can help them overcome or avoid frustration. "Jason you are working so well on this. What you've done so far is spot on, keep it up."

ii. Avoid personal judgements

We've already discovered that praise can make some students dependent on the adult giving the praise and that they can modify their behaviour solely to please the teacher. This is particularly common when a statement of praise involving a personal judgement from the teacher is directed to a power-oriented student - when they see the person giving the praise as the person with all the power, there is a conflict. Rather than judging students by telling them what we think of their efforts we should be encouraging them to reflect on their own efforts. The following statements illustrate my meaning:

"I think you've done a great job" is a judgement which encourages the student to be dependent on the view of the teacher whereas "You've done a great job" encourages independence and self motivation.

"I really like what you've done here" is a judgement which encourages the student to be dependent on the view of the teacher

whereas "You should be proud of what you've done here" encourages independence and self motivation.

"You're my best student" is a judgement which encourages the student to be dependent on the view of the teacher whereas "You work really hard in this class" encourages independence and self motivation.

iii. Be sincere

Most students can recognise fake praise from a hundred yards away - and they don't like it. If you can't say it with honesty, it's best not to say anything at all. Remember: praise comes from the heart, flattery comes from the teeth.

iv. Be aware that praise is often more effective on a 1:1 basis

Some students (a surprisingly large proportion) don't like receiving praise in front of other people. For whatever reason – some just can't accept compliments very well - you have more chance of your praise being well-received if you give it out of earshot of the rest of the students. Catch them on the way out of the door or call them over to a quiet corner of the room. Praise is much more sincere when it's a private affair.

v. Make it specific

When you praise a child you make them feel your appreciation by telling them exactly WHAT they did and WHY it was good. True praise comes from genuinely noticing when they put effort into something or have managed to complete something they wouldn't normally manage. Giving thoughtful attention to a student's work demonstrates that you recognise their work or improved behaviour.

"Paul, stand back and look at what you've done... this is a fantastic portrait! What is really impressive is the way you've made that eye come to life by showing the light reflecting here. That really makes it come alive!"

"Paul, you've done so well. You've sat quietly for the last 10 minutes and got on with your work. That's great because I've been able to go and help other students and I haven't needed to shout at you. Well done!"

Don't those examples sound better than *"very good, Paul"*?

vi. Make them reflect on their efforts

Some people lavish praise on students for literally anything and everything in the hope that a torrent of positive words will raise their self esteem and motivate them. "Wow, I love the way you closed the door there!"

In order to develop intrinsic motivation in a task we should be getting students to reflect on what they've done. By getting them to stop and think about their efforts we encourage them to recognise and evaluate the positive feelings associated with positive action. If they enjoy these feelings, there is more chance they will want to repeat the actions – for themselves, and not just to please someone else.

"What do you think of what you've done?"

"How does it feel to have got over that difficult problem?"

Praise strategies

In addition to direct praise, here are four more very powerful praise strategies you might not have used. Most have an odd name just to make them sound more ingenious and complicated than they actually are – 'Windscreen wiper praise', 'Ego praise' and 'Stealth praise'. I know, 'written praise' does sound positively dull by comparison!

1) Windscreen wiper praise

Proximity praise relies on the 'ripple effect' where the positive feelings from praising individual students who are working hard or behaving well spread or 'ripple' around the room; other students get the message that if they behave in a similar way, they too will receive praise. We can multiply the power of this effect with a novel praise idea which someone suggested on one of our live classroom management courses. It's called 'windscreen wiper praise'; it's very straightforward but does need a brief explanation.

Let's say you have a student ('Damien') who is off-task and not working as he should be. The idea is to subtly but repeatedly praise the students sitting on either side of him - 'Kyle' and 'Kieran' - for their work and/or behaviour. If Kyle and Kieran are friends of Damien it will make this even more effective but it works well even if they aren't. This is one possible scenario:

"Hey Kieran you've got it. I honestly didn't think you'd manage that question; absolutely brilliant - it's good to see you learning."

"Let's have a look at yours Kyle...you've really improved. You've got that bit right, well done. Now, how could you improve this bit and get to the next level?"

A few minutes later...

"Thank you for putting that in the bin Kyle. By the way I saw that film last night you were talking about - it was really funny, thanks for suggesting it."

"Nice one Kieran. I like what you've done there. I'm really pleased with you two, you're working very well, thank you."

Do you see how it works and where the name 'windscreen wiper praise' comes from? By continually engaging with Kyle and Kieran in a positive manner Damien's head will be going from side to side wondering what his two neighbours have done to attract all this attention. Students generally like getting attention - especially if it's positive - and by NOT giving Damien attention but instead giving it to his neighbours we take the power of proximity praise to the next level. Another plus to this method is that it works equally well in wet or dry weather.

2) Ego praise

This is a great way to acknowledge a student's strengths, abilities and efforts without saying anything to them directly. Some students, as we know, find it difficult to accept praise directly – this gets round the problem.

"Go and ask Jonathan about it – he's picked this up very quickly."

"Go and watch Alan for a minute – he's brilliant at this and you can learn a lot from him."

(Both statements would be spoken just loud enough for Jonathan and Alan to hear).

3) Stealth praise

This is another type of indirect praise (don't worry, it does not involve sneaking up behind students in soft-soled shoes). This time, you report the student's efforts and abilities to another member of staff just within earshot of the student, as if you're not aware they are listening. Students love to discover that staff talk positively about them:

"Did you see what Alan did this morning Mr Smith? Honestly, I can't believe how hard that lad is trying; what a turn-around."

Here's one more...

4) Written Praise

Sending a short, positive letter home can transform a previously negative child - literally overnight - into one who is motivated and eager to please. This is also one method that works well even with older students, right up to age 16 and beyond. It is also very effective for students who don't accept public praise very well - a letter home means their friends will never find out!

Letters home can be 'quick-notes' or more formal, traditional letters on school headed paper. You can send out simple postcards for odd pieces of particularly good work or award 'extra special' letters in response to sustained effort.

Power Strategy #5:

Written feedback

Teacher feedback is another potentially powerful motivational tool. Since your comments, marks and grades can have a huge impact on your learners' confidence and enthusiasm, you need to make sure it is as constructive and effective as possible.

Written feedback is usually given in one of three ways – scores (percentages, marks out of ten or grades such as A, B, C etc), written comments, and both scores and comments together. There is a surprising difference not only in the way these three types of feedback are interpreted by students but also in the effects they have on their motivation and attitude.

In general, grades are only motivational to those who get good ones. How would you feel if every time you got your book back from the teacher it had a big red 'F' on it or a low score like 30-40%. Pretty unmotivated, right? Certainly, your attitude to learning would be a lot different to students who got the 'A's & 'B's.

Conversely, written comments can have a positive effect on all students at all stages on the ability spectrum – providing they are written in the right manner (and we'll deal with that in a second).

I recently heard about an interesting study recently (I'm afraid I don't have the details) in which the effects of 'written comments versus grades and scores on student motivation/attitude' were tested. Some students were given written comments on their work, some were given scores/grades and some were given both written comments and grades. As predicted, the majority of students who were given written comments were found to have a positive attitude towards the work they had done. For those given grades alone, those with the highest grades (A's and B's or high percentages) had a more positive attitude to the work while those given low grades had a largely negative attitude.

What do you think happened to those given both written comments and grades?

Interestingly, the results showed that the written comments had virtually no effect on student motivation. It seemed that they didn't even bother to read the comment – their level of motivation was entirely dependent on the grade they received instead. This was a case of 'what grade did I get?' and that was it. The written comment wasn't even read.

What can we take from this?

Whenever possible it may be prudent to add a written comment to student work instead of a grade – particularly for low-achieving students who may be adversely affected by a low score. There are certain times when scores and grades need to be shared with students, but the message from this study would suggest that a well structured written comment can have a far more positive affect on your students' attitudes to work.

Three factors to improve written feedback:

i. Make it prompt. Return tests, assignments, books and papers promptly.

ii. Acknowledge achievements made. Tell them what they have done right.

iii. Tell them how to improve. Give them a small step they can take to improve their work further:

A simple A-B-C template for effective feedback:

This simple template makes it easy to structure your feedback:

A: Acknowledge what they've done right.

B: Praise them for what they've done right.

C: Give them a small step to take next in order to improve.

"You have done this right (A), well done (B). Now, this is what you need to do next for more success...(C)"

Example:

"Excellent Jonny, you've got all your full stops in place. Well done lad, you're really taking notice today. To make your work even better from now on you need to make sure you put a capital letter at the start of every new sentence."

Power Strategy #6:

Challenge refusals respectfully

"Our response has crucial consequences ... it can create a climate of compliance or defiance, a mood of contentment or contention, a desire to make amends or to take revenge."

(Chesterton, 1924)

We have to remember that students who aren't motivated to work during our lessons may well be victims of the demotivators we mentioned in 'Why your students are NOT motivated'. It is worth remembering this when we have to confront refusers, disrupters and 'don't-try-hard-enoughers'.

Responding to these students by nagging and threatening never works; if anything it's only going to make matters worse. A better way is to focus first on any positive – even the smallest thing that they have done right – such as turning up for the lesson, walking without getting their legs tangled up, or managing to write their name on their paper.

Go in negatively with a student who isn't performing as you would like, and a barrier shoots up, the student hides behind it and closes his ears. They don't want to be nagged, they don't want to be reprimanded - so they either retaliate and argue, or simply shut down.

Let me tell you a story to illustrate what I mean...

A couple of years ago I was delivering a training course to the non-teaching staff at a large English comprehensive school, one of whom (a caretaker) told me that the students at the school had no respect whatsoever for the staff. He told me he was routinely ridiculed, ignored, and (if he ever confronted a student for a minor offence such as dropping litter) subjected to verbal abuse. He was understandably very frustrated about this situation, and the rest of the staff – cleaners, library staff, catering staff and support workers - all agreed that the students were 'out of control' with no respect at all for staff.

I wanted, naturally, to know more; I wanted to know if this really was always the case. Had there been any instances of students responding respectfully and if so, what had the member of staff done, how had this result been achieved?

"Surely they don't abuse you all the time. You seem like a very friendly, jovial man to me. We had a caretaker just like you when I was a boy at school and we all loved him, he was so much fun. Surely you get occasions when the kids are on your side and do as you ask?" (This man had, throughout the whole morning, had us all in fits of laughter with some of his comments and wisecracks so I knew his personality would appeal to many of the students).

He sat back with his arms folded and a smile crept onto his face. "Aye, there have been a few to be honest when I think about it." He went on to tell us all a short story which I have used on virtually all my training courses ever since because, to me, it highlights perfectly how important it is that we challenge students **in the right manner** when they are doing something wrong.

He told us about a group of year 10 boys (15 year olds to non-UK readers) who routinely played football (soccer to non-UK readers) at the side of one of the buildings. There was always a pile of litter to clear up after their game, which the boys left behind of course, and there had been several instances of staff cars being scratched or damaged. There had also been, in fact, a spate of broken windows.

The caretaker had been instructed by the Head teacher to move the boys on from this area whenever he saw them there and this was where all his frustrations lay. He said that when he normally told them to 'clear off' and take their ball to the playing fields he was met with a tirade of abuse. He had grown to dread break times because of this. He said his normal reaction to the boys went something like this:

"Oi! What do you think you're playing at? Think for once! You're going to break a window if you play here and then I'll have to sort it out and clear up the mess! Take your ball and clear off!"

To which the boys replied *"**** off!"*

But on this occasion, purely by chance, he approached them in a totally different way. He had watched one of the boys perform a touch of football magic as he weaved in and out of the other players before sending a shot screaming past the keeper into the makeshift goal. Being a football fanatic himself he was suitably impressed and couldn't contain himself.

"Shot! Hey, that was a hell of a goal, nice one!" he shouted and all the boys turned towards him.

They were taken aback and... they were <u>listening</u>. The scorer was smiling. Suddenly, in that moment, there was some affinity and connection.

The caretaker continued:

"Hey lads, can I have a word? Listen, when you play football here there's a chance the windows will get broken and cars will get damaged. I'm the one who has to clear up and I don't want to be on your backs all the time – I'm sick of it to be honest. I know you enjoy your game and I don't want to stop you playing because I like football too but can you do me a favour and take your ball round that corner on the field? You can play there no problem."

To his surprise the boys were enthusiastic in their replies and moved on without the usual abuse. When any of these boys saw him in the corridors from that day on they greeted him with a smile and a polite *"hello Sir".*

When we start conversations off with something positive there is more chance students will listen. Many of them are so accustomed to being reprimanded that as soon as they hear negative words they shut down, the barriers lock in place.

I hear you think, 'what does this have to do with motivation?' Well, everything.

We're talking here about meeting your students' needs for power. How empowering is it to be shouted at, criticised, or nagged at - especially when it happens in front of your friends?

Imagine you have a class of challenging students to teach (yes, another!) and today is the day they are supposed to bring in completed homework. The example I'm going to use is a group of 14 year olds but the same idea holds true for any age.

Scenario #1

You walk in the room and the students are out of their seats, chatting with each other. You want to get the lesson started so you shout for quiet.

"Quiet please, let's get started!"

Nobody seems to hear you, or if they do they choose not to respond; you are ignored. You try again with a "come on, quiet please!". A few students look up and then turn away. You almost had them, but right now you're not important. You try a different tack and go to some of the tables where students are huddled. Even when you're up close you still have to shout to make yourself heard and they just glance at you with disgust. They are out of control, and your only option is to yell at the top of your voice.

"SHUT UP!" In the shocked silence you continue. "I've had enough! I'm sick of you not listening to me! Let's get one thing straight, when you're in my room you listen to me! GOT IT?"

The students casually turn to face you and slump into their chairs. Clearly they are enjoying the show. A loud raspberry comes from the back of the room.

"I try my best to help you all and I get nothing back from you. Nothing! Now, while I'm on the subject of getting things back from you, get your homework out."

Some students grin, others give each other the 'this is going to get even more exciting' look. Nobody has brought homework, of course.

"Put your hand up if you've done your homework. Not one person. NOT ONE PERSON! Why should I bother? Why should I bother putting my effort in for you lot if you can't be bothered to try? You know what, I get paid whether you lot pass or you don't, it doesn't matter one bit to me. If you want to carry on failing that's fine, it's your choice."

From that point on comments such as "Urgh, you don't even care, what sort of teacher are you?", "You should teach us better", "Charming!" and "Can we go home then?" fill the room.

You leave the room at the end of the lesson feeling like a wrung-out dish cloth, relieved that you don't have to see this class for another 48 hours. Oh, the joys of teaching! Have you had days like that?

Now let's look at a different way of approaching the same situation and see how a different approach can create a very different outcome.

This approach is centred on relationships and respect. While the emphasis of this programme is chiefly on preventing motivation problems by meeting student needs it is also important not to compromise those needs when responding to problems, giving students direction, and addressing problems such as low motivation.

Scenario #2

This time you are in the room before the students so you're able to greet them at the door – a very important point and often overlooked. The few minutes outside a classroom provide a golden opportunity to cement bonds with students and set the tone you want in the room. You greet all of them by name, asking them how they are and making sure you make reference to their individual interests, home lives and character traits.

"Hi Jonny, how did the rugby match go this weekend? Did you score this week?"

"Hey Gemma, love the shoes! Spending your mum's money again or have you got your Saturday job back?"

With those students who have issues they'd rather not share with the group, you are more subtle but no less interested in them.

(Quietly, out of ear-shot of the other students) "How did it go at your dad's this weekend Brian? Everything OK?"

You've also had the forethought to arrange the tables a little differently today because you know you're going to have to tackle the issue of incomplete homework. It has been getting out of control so you want to nip the problem in the bud. The tables are arranged in a horseshoe shape with all chairs facing your desk.

You ask the students to sit down facing the front and tell them you need them to be very quiet, because you've got something important to share with them. Your choice of words so far creates sufficient intrigue to have them following your instructions.

You sit on your desk facing the group and wait patiently, smiling, for them to settle down. With some groups the 'waiting patiently' tactic doesn't work – you could wait all lesson and they'd just laugh at you but you've worked hard with this group to build an atmosphere of mutual trust over the last few months so they are respectfully compliant.

You begin.

"Okay, welcome everyone, it's great to see my favourite group as usual." You smile cheerfully. *"Can I ask you to put your hand up if you have brought your homework in today, as I asked?"*

Three hands slowly rise.

"Thank you to the three of you, you've made me very proud. But... the rest of you... haven't made me proud. In fact you've made me worried and upset."

"Awww, poor sir!" comes a shout from the back, and everyone laughs.

"That's very kind Jonny but hear me out, please. Now, put your hand up if you can tell me why a teacher, or why 'I', would be worried and upset just because some of my class don't bring their homework in?"

There are numerous silly remarks in response to this but you continue.

"I'll tell you why. I'm worried because I want you all to do well. I'm worried because I can see what will happen if you carry on like this and it would upset me to see you a few years down the line with no job, no money, no fancy car, no nice clothes, an out-of-date iphone. Get the picture? Okay then. I'll tell you what we can do to prevent this disappointing vision of the future coming true. We'll work together to find a solution to our homework problem. Who wants to start us off? Who can give me a reason – any reason at all - why homework isn't getting done? I'll write them down on the board as you sing them out."

Gradually the students start to get involved and before long they are all keen to voice their concerns and contribute. You write up their thoughts and, after around fifteen minutes you draw the discussion to a close.

"Okay folks, some great suggestions there, thank you. This is good stuff, we can work with this. One of the biggest issues seems to be that you find the work confusing and don't understand what you're supposed to do. You also say you haven't time to get it done in two days, and sometimes you just forget.

How about this then? I'll agree to make some changes when I set the work so that it is fully explained and there is no confusion. I'll also give you all a session on time management and give you some funky ways of finding extra time in your busy schedules. That way the work gets done without causing you any inconvenience. In return, you all agree to spend two hours on your homework this week and get it in for Friday. Everyone agree?"

Students motivated by power need to be treated with respect. They are the quickest to complain if they perceive they are being patronised or mistreated. This method above may not work for every student – there are going to be some who still lack the motivation to complete their work or take part in lessons but that's to be expected – but we're wise enough to know we can't please all students all the time. One thing is certain though - it is going to bring more positive results than the first method, and maintains our needs-focused setting from which we can apply further strategies.

Assignment 3:

1) Responsibility: Consider using any or all of the five methods to give students more responsibility.

Buddy Schemes: Provide a structured format for one or more of your unmotivated students to help another student.

Offer a challenging student or group of students the opportunity to teach a future lesson.

Assign roles and jobs to challenging students.

Allow students choice in the type of activities you will include next lesson.

2) Opportunity to succeed: Ensure students are given adequate opportunities to experience success.

Use the five point plan in Power Strategy #2 in lessons.

3) Help Students set goals: Teach students how to set their own achievable goals and targets.

Arrange 1:1 sessions with select students or teach students as a group how to set their goals using the questions in Power Strategy #3. Review these goals with them on a regular basis.

4) Recognition: Use effective praise strategies to give positive recognition for students' efforts.

Use the six points to make praise more effective in conjunction with the praise strategies outlines in Power Strategy #4 to recognise student effort in and out of lessons.

5) Use written comments in feedback: Mark books, assignments and homework using written comments.

Whenever possible, mark work promptly and use the simple template for effective written feedback in Power Strategy #5.

Strategies to Satisfy the Need for Fun

Fun Strategy #1:

Create Intrigue

By creating some intrigue we can often win round students who have preconceived notions that the lesson won't interest them; **we invite attention rather than demanding** it. Intrigue can be created simply by making any change to the norm, as these examples show:

• changes to the physical environment (room layout, the seating, the lighting);

• changes to the type of lesson tasks on offer or the way information is usually delivered;

• visitors/outside speakers, who can give students a (welcome) break from your boring old voice ;

• equipment or demonstrations set up before students enter (The more dramatic the better);

• changes to your own appearance or delivery style (here's your chance to get your fancy dress kit out of the cupboard!)

Here are two more ways of creating intrigue in lessons:

• **Intrigue idea #1: Use Props**

Tangible props are a 'never-fail' attention grabber, particularly when they are abstract or novel and are presented in a creative way such as the example below (mystery bag). They can also be used to amuse and entertain, keep the mood upbeat and break the monotony of teacher-talk and demonstrations (think Elvis wig or clown's nose). Additionally, they can be used as an aid to learning to make explanations easier to understand, focus attention and demonstrate abstract concepts in a visual and concrete way.

One of the most interesting props I've ever had the privilege to use in a lesson was a genuine relic from the Titanic. No, not Kate Winslet - but a broken pocket watch belonging to a young bellboy on one of the first class lifts, before he tragically drowned.

My students had been working on their research project for a few weeks and were fascinated by the whole Titanic story. To see this piece of living history up close, after previously only having access to pictures, videos and reference books and that awful drone by Celine Dion, was simply amazing for them. They had already discovered the exact time the ship was documented as taking her final plunge - 2:20am – and had filled this time in as the last entry on their time lines. When they saw that the watch had actually stopped at precisely 2:20am, they were, understandably, completely spellbound. It was a tremendous example of how powerful props can be, and a great ice breaker for getting the lesson going.

Obviously this was a one-off. The chances of getting your hands on priceless relics are slim and any efforts to procure them from your local museum may not be viewed favourably. I was lucky as a friend of mine knew the lady who owned the watch (and several other artifacts). She had never shown them to anyone outside her home up to that point but was thrilled to be able to enhance the children's education by coming in to school to display them. I was lucky indeed, but we all have friends and relatives and you never know, it's possible that one of them has, or knows someone who has, a suitable prop for your next lesson.

Subject-related props can literally bring a subject to life. As an introduction to a lesson they can grab attention like nothing else. The Titanic watch, for example, was actually introduced to the group through the activity described below – 'Mystery Bag'.

When the students entered the room, the bag (one of the original sacks used by the authorities to hold passengers' belongings retrieved after the accident) was waiting ominously on the centre table. They were instantly attracted to it and were desperate to find out what it was. Job done; we had their attention.

The Mystery Bag activity is a tried and tested way to introduce a prop. You won't be able to use it every lesson but as a one-off method to get attention it takes some beating with any age-group.

Mystery Bag

Number of people: Unlimited

Age group: Any

Materials: Prop related to the lesson content together with a suitable bag or container.
Time: 10 minutes

Overview:

A lesson-related prop is hidden in a bag or container. Students have to guess what's inside. Younger students may enjoy this as a regular routine ("What's in the bag today?") but for older students it should only be used occasionally. It relies on intrigue and falls flat if the prop doesn't live up to the hype which the game naturally generates.

Directions:

1. Write on the board 'You have 20 chances to guess what's in the bag'.

2. Explain to students that they can volunteer to ask a question to try and determine what's in the bag. Questions can only be those which have a 'yes' or 'no' answer, ie they can ask "is it blue?" but not "what colour is it?"

3. Write their questions down on the board one at a time to keep track of the total number asked and to avoid repeated questions. Answer them "yes" or "no" and put a tick or a cross next to the question. (I always like to have two noise effects for right and wrong answers to add to the humorous atmosphere - a kazoo or duck call for wrong answers

and a bugle horn or quiz master's bell for right answers. Be sure to carry an even-tempered duck if you choose this route.)

4. Tension mounts once their questions are into double figures as they realise they might not succeed – particularly when you tell them they will get extra homework if they don't get the right answer.

• **Intrigue idea #2: Present tasks in envelopes.** It's surprising how much intrigue can be built up with nothing more expensive or creative than an envelope with 'Mission Instructions' written on it, handed to students as they enter. We all love to receive letters and parcels through the post - the unknown contents creating fascination and appeal - which makes this humble piece of stationery the ideal delivery boy for a host of quick, intrigue-inducing activities. Here are two variations on the same theme:

Envelope Idea #1:

Spot the mistake

Materials: Pre-written cards or pictures sealed in envelopes.

Time: 15-20 minutes.

Overview: This activity can be adapted for any curriculum area. Mistake cards could be sentences which don't make sense, a paragraph with errors in it, a recipe with steps missing and wrong quantities, a sample of a student's work needing correction, a picture with key parts omitted/blanked out, MP's expenses claim etc.

Directions:

1. Arrange ten to twelve envelopes with a selection of 'mistakes' – one sample in each envelope. Number the envelopes 1 to 12.

2. Students form diverse groups (see **Power Strategies**) of three or four and are each given a sheet of paper with the numbers one to

twelve (or however many envelopes there are) written down the left hand side.

3. The envelopes are placed on a table at the front of the room and one member from each team takes any one envelope back to their team mates. As a group, each team finds the mistakes and each team member writes the answers on their sheets next to the relevant number.

4. One person in the team is nominated as 'counter' and counts the mistake cards back into the envelope before replacing it on the front table and taking another envelope. This is repeated until the teams have completed all the envelopes.

Envelope Idea #2:

Scavenger Hunt

Overview: This activity can be adapted for any curriculum area and is tremendous fun. It is also another 'set and forget' type of activity during which the students effectively become self-watering plants. In diverse teams, where peer support naturally occurs, they work to solve the clues, find facts and collate information. Clues can be solved by gathering information online, from offline resources or from a mixture of the two.

The more time you spend setting this up, and the more creative you are with your clues, the more enjoyment your students will get. The only problem with this activity is that your students will want to do it again and again!

Directions:

1. Teacher identifies websites and offline resources such as books, wall displays, relevant experts, newspaper articles etc together with one specific fact/answer relevant to each source. Questions are constructed for each fact and written on a question/clue sheet.

An extra interactive dimension can be brought into the scavenger hunt by planting some clues around school rather than merely listing them as questions on the question/clue sheet. Budding Sherlocks will be led to find this clue as a result of solving the preceding clue.

For example:

(On the question sheet):

1. In the library on the wall there is a leaflet from the Vegan Society. Write three sentences from the leaflet which suggest dairy farming is cruel.

You will find your next clue under the table directly underneath the leaflet.

Role-play and Drama

For younger children role-play is a vital part of their education. It gives opportunities to play through and practise a wide range of real-life situations whilst gaining experience and practising skills in areas such as problem solving, language and communication, numeracy, reasoning, listening etc.

For older students role-play is, again, very useful and powerful for developing social skills and also for dealing with a wide range of potentially embarrassing or sensitive social development issues such as peer pressure, drugs, bullying, race, sex, relationships etc. It allows them to explore their views and responses in a risk-free environment.

Most students really enjoy role-play, once they get into it. I always remember John, one of the most challenging 14 year old students I've ever taught. He wouldn't listen, wouldn't sit still in his seat, was abusive and disruptive to other students and was totally negative towards any and all tasks put in front of him. He had been thrown out of mainstream school because he was unable to cope.

One day I discovered he had a passion for acting. This normally abusive and aggressive individual, totally disinterested in normal school life suddenly took on a whole new persona once this skill had awoken in him. He absolutely loved getting up in front of everyone in role-plays and skits, and was perfectly well behaved when given the opportunity to do so. It was as if he needed a 'fix'. So from that day on, whenever I took the opportunity to involve him and the rest of the class in a role-play activity he was a happy lad. If you are plagued by reluctant learners perhaps some of them will benefit from role-play activities.

Role-play activities - from the simplest thirty-second sketch right to a full-blown mini-play complete with costumes and props - are exciting and above all, FUN for many students and can be used to bring a dynamic, active element to lessons. Dull material can be transformed into a practical and enjoyable activity and students can be given an experience which is often hard to forget.

Tips for incorporating drama into lessons

Drama tip #1: Avoid too much repetition

Having the whole class carry out the same role-play (e.g. exploring an emotive issue such as a bullying scenario) in their respective groups at the same time is a good way to make sure all students gain experience and skills associated with taking part. However, while it is beneficial for students to watch other groups perform, it would be unfair to expect them to sit through the same play time after time. It is far better to create slight variations on a theme and change the scenario slightly for each group.

Drama tip #2: Engage the audience

A potential drawback of role-play is that audience members are often expected to sit for too long watching other students performing, and this can lead to boredom and misbehaviour. One way of including all members of the class – even those who aren't involved in a particular performance – is to occasionally stop the play and give audience members the chance to replace one of the actors, giving an alternative course of action for the performance. This is particularly useful where there might be more than one point of view in a scenario; 'rewinding' the play and 'replaying' with a new actor who has a different agenda is an excellent way for students to fully explore an issue/topic. (Film directors working with Keanu Reeves often wish they could do this.)

Another way to engage the audience is to make sure they have something specific to watch out for throughout the performance. Some students will benefit from being given a question sheet the answers to which will be found by watching the play; while others may just need pointers such as 'make a note of all the different ways Simon offers support to his friend'.

Drama tip #3: Have everyone participate

For some students role-play can be quite daunting and they will try to opt out. Making participation compulsory will turn some of them off straight away. Instead, encourage everyone to take part in the planning and those who express concern at performing can be told they can have a non-speaking part. If they later want to speak, they can do so. Many students find, once they get over their initial fear, that they really enjoy role-play activities and will actively request bigger roles in the next session. One of my students who flatly refused to take part in the Christmas play eventually ended up having three parts. Once he'd got over his initial fear he found he loved getting up in front of an audience; and there's absolutely no stopping him now!

Drama tip #4: Include a debrief session

Like any inquiry-based exercise, role-playing needs to be followed by a debriefing in which the students can define and reinforce what they have learned. This can be handled in reflective writing or in a class discussion and provides essential feedback for improving future sessions – 'what worked well/didn't work well?'.

Drama tip #5: Assess their efforts

Generally, grades are given for written projects associated with the role-play, but presentations and even involvement in interactive exercises can also be graded. Special considerations for grading in role-playing exercises include:

• Playing in character - working to further the character's goals and making statements that reflect the character's perspective.

• Being constructive, courteous and showing empathy and understanding for the views of others.

Remember to use the pointers on feedback in Power Strategy #.5

Suitable Drama Activities

Drama activity 1:

Acting content

This strategy can be used where you might normally explain a concept through teacher-talk, video or handout. Instead, the students learn by discovery – by 'experiencing' the actual idea and by actually 'becoming' the content. Virtually any concept or topic can be taught in this way with some creative thought.

Example #1: As a five-minute introduction to Particle Theory, the behaviour of atoms can be illustrated and experienced by putting students into groups and having them behave as particles do in the three states – solid, liquid and gas. In their solid state the students would be stood closely together in a tight group, shaking slightly or vibrating. As liquids the distance between each student would be increased and they would move around to fill a designated area. They may hold on to each other to signify occasional bonding whilst vibrating and moving more rapidly. As gases the students would move freely round the room, filling the entire space and occasionally colliding with each other. (Care obviously needed – don't get them too drunk!)

Singing content

'The Ron Clark Story' starring Matthew Perry (from 'Friends') is an inspirational film which every teacher can gain much from; there are some great ideas and emotive messages throughout.

One of the ideas mentioned which you may have also used is to have students sing and dance their way through lesson content in order to make it memorable and enjoyable. The way this was done by Mr Clark when he committed all the presidents of the USA to a rap and sang it to his class was highly amusing to watch, but when the students took the stage to do their raps the real reasons for the activity became apparent: although they had covered the same lesson content earlier and hated it, they absolutely loved doing this activity - and they successfully learned the content.

It always surprises me how much young people love to sing – especially the reluctant learners. Being given the option of writing their own subject-based lyrics to their favourite tunes is a guaranteed winner in the classroom. You can also find ready-made lyrics and songs for a huge number of lesson topics by typing '"name of topic" song' into Google, eg "Rock Cycle" song.

Drama activity 3:

Mini-plays

We don't have time to produce full-blown plays complete with props and sets as described below but there are opportunities for mini-plays in every lesson. They are a powerful teaching aid and a natural active learning method – much better and more memorable than teacher-talk or videos.

Example #1: Let students take on the roles of characters from a book they are studying and allow other members of the class to question them about their background, their thoughts, their actions and their intentions.

Example #2: Split the class into groups and have each group perform a short sketch (five minutes maximum) that depicts one of the events from the lesson topic. All students in each group would be involved in researching and writing scripts as well as rehearsing and performing.

Drama activity 4:

Full plays

The resources, time and energy required to script and run a full-blown play in a lesson means this is a very occasional activity but it really should be considered as a possibility simply because it is such a powerful learning opportunity.

Plays for many units of study can actually be purchased in a ready-made format but in many cases it may be better to write your own. A well-written play will become one of your best teaching resources, something you can use again and again, year after year, to engage and delight your students.

• Plan your play well in advance. There should be sufficient parts for everyone to have at least some stage time.

• Run auditions for parts at the start of the topic/unit of study.

• Have students help source props.

• Run rehearsals as a starter to your normal lessons so that the play will be well known by the time you finish the unit of study.

• Consider adding songs to make your play a musical – kids love to sing.

• Use the play as a grand finale to your unit of study.

Drama activity 5:

Assessment tools

Acting can be an incredibly effective assessment tool – certainly a nice change from the usual mini-test.

When students have learned key facts one of the best ways to get them to remember those facts or pieces of information is to have them actively involved in using the information. The following examples show creative ways of having students use the information they've learned in a role-play activity which serves as an effective assessment method.

Example #1: Students are taught the names of bones in the human skeleton. As their plenary they must take the role of surgeon and perform 'operations' on their learning partner – identifying named broken bones.

Example #2: Students are put into groups of four with one member of each group acting as the talk show host. Each 'guest' can then be invited to speak on a given topic.

This is a great way to review a book the class has been studying, with each 'guest' acting as a character in the book and giving their own story when invited by the host.

Drama activity 6:

TV Programme

Students love this activity and the format can be adapted to virtually any subject area. The three programme types I have used with success are 'Children's TV Show', 'TV Quiz Show' and 'The News'.

Example: Students split into groups of four or five. For 'The News' one or two students act as the main presenters, explaining key points from the lesson/subject content while another group member could act as a roving reporter to present 'breaking news' or 'on the ground' reports from key people/experts in the field.

Drama activity 7:

Filming

Filming covers a wide range of learning objectives and can enhance any role-play or drama session. Activity 6 above lends itself perfectly to filming and the students love watching their finished products at the end of the session. Here are some tips to get the most from filming:

• Consider filming different aspects of the plot in different locations/rooms to give variety.

• Try and keep video sessions short and snappy. Encourage students to break their presentation up into 'scenes'.

• Encourage a question and answer session at the end of the presentation and film that too.

• As a humorous extra, allow students to include their funny 'out-takes' at the end of the show.

Fun Strategy #3:

Make Learning Active

Active learning gets students engaged in the material being studied through reading, writing, discussing, listening, and reflecting. A growing body of research has made it clear that motivation in lessons (as well as the quality of teaching and learning) is improved when students have opportunities to clarify, question, apply, and consolidate new knowledge through paired/group discussions, role-plays, structured cooperative learning and problem solving. We've already looked specifically at role-plays above, and we covered cooperative group work in our 'Belonging Strategies', so let's look at a few additional ways to make learning more active:

Active Teaching Strategy #1:

Mini Reviews

Mini Reviews can be used to inject some energy into the lesson at any stage and are a very effective way to reinforce any piece of learning. Students remember very little from a lesson if they only hear the information – possibly as little as 10%. When they are given the chance to repeat it, this figure increases dramatically.

• **Mini Review #1: Star Jumps**

1. Ask the whole class to stand up and assume the shape of a star (as in 'star jump' – legs apart, arms apart reaching upwards).

2. Tell them they can't move until someone shouts out one topic-related important piece of information they've picked up from the lesson or previous lessons.

3. As soon as someone shouts something relevant, everyone jumps to the second phase of a star jump – legs together, hands down by sides.

4. Repeat the process until everyone has completed about ten jumps.

• **Mini Review #2: Joggers**

1. Ask the whole class to stand up.

2. Ask a student to call out a number between one and twenty (or between one and ten – you'll see why it might be best to reduce this number in a moment). This is the 'target number'.

3. Start the students jogging on the spot.

4. Students have to continue jogging on the spot until sufficient (depending on the target number) relevant, topic-related facts have been called out.

• **Mini Review #3: Fireworks**

Tell students that a 'firework' is what you call it when a student jumps up from their seat and contributes something positive to the lesson, eg by stating what they've learned so far or how they plan to use that information. Start a timer and tell students you need to see fifteen 'fireworks' in the next 60 seconds. Sometimes an incentive may be helpful:

"Okay, it's break time in ten minutes but if you want your break I need to see fifteen fireworks in the next sixty seconds."

Active Teaching Strategy #2:

Teach-Backs

Teach-back activities are fun ways to encourage students to cement their learning by teaching others what they have been taught – by demonstrating, explaining and (wait for it...) teaching! Remember the saying 'You never really learn anything until you teach it'?

As well as helping students learn new information, teach-back activities are great for the teacher too because they let you check for understanding and see how much your students have learned. They also give you a bit of free time (remember that?).

Ready, Steady... TEACH!

No materials required. This is a ritual or routine to build up with your students which can be used as a quick (and often extremely lively) review at the end of any phase of teacher-talk or explanation. It is as effective as it is simple.

You explain to your students that whenever you call out the words (in your best Ainsley Harriot voice) "Ready, Steady... TEACH!" they are to work with their allotted learning partner for thirty seconds to a minute to teach back what they have learned moments before.

Learning partners should be numbered one and two because this Teach-Back has three phases.

Phase one: After teaching the group the new information the teacher asks if there are any questions before moving on in order to clarify the learning and eliminate misunderstandings during the next stage.

Phase two: The teacher calls "Ready, Steady... TEACH!" and partner one immediately starts teaching partner two the new concept. It is important that they are encouraged to over-emphasise the key points with facial expressions and exaggerated hand gestures (humour makes learning stick) and that they move through the information quickly. For a difficult concept students are given up to a minute to teach back the key points of the new information but it is best to keep the activity brief – once partners lose interest, the effect is lost. This should be a fast-paced, brief review, nothing more.

Phase three: The teacher calls 'come in number one, your time is up' (or something similar) to bring the first session of teaching to a close and have partners swap roles. On the second call of "Ready, Steady... TEACH!" partner two teaches partner one. Partners then thank each other for being wonderful teachers and the lesson continues.

The Four Musketeers

Overview: The motto of the Three Musketeers was 'all for one and one for all.' This activity has a similar principle in that team members work together for the good of the group. It's different in that -students form groups of four rather than only three!

Directions:

1. Students form diverse groups of four where possible.

2. Teacher reads out a question and gives a few minutes for students to work individually and write an answer down.

3. Teacher gives 'discussion time' for students to discuss their answers with the rest of their group members. Students are encouraged to help each other during this phase so that everyone's answer is improved and everyone has a good understanding.

4. Teacher calls 'time' and picks a number between one and four. The relevant student answers the question for the benefit of the class using the combined knowledge of his/her team mates.

Active Teaching Strategy #3:

Games and Energisers

Games and energisers help provide the essential 'fun' element to the lesson experience and are a great way to infuse a lesson with positive emotion and interaction. They can also be a life saver during those daunting times when a lesson starts to go wrong, providing a mood-changing diversion from certain classroom chaos. They also give your learners a chance to interact closely with their peers as they share the highs and lows of the game experience, allowing for strong bonding and community-building.

As well as all this (and this is an incredibly important point) games provide an arena in which social skills can be learned and practised. We can't 'tell' a person to have better social skills and we can't 'make' them get on with other people. They have to learn for themselves the benefits of doing so. Students soon learn that the only way they will be able to participate in a fun activity or game is by playing by the rules and by using appropriate social skills which they are then able to draw on in a variety of real-life situations.

Interactive whiteboards and other technological advances have taken classroom games into a new dimension but we must not forget the important role that simple, traditional learning games, such as quizzes, play in social and educational development.

• Sample Game: Pub Quiz

Overview: An active and fun review activity with a competitive element. The 'rounds' of this quiz (with scoring for each round) help keep students attentive throughout the whole quiz. Having students in diverse (mixed ability) teams helps include weaker students who may feel excluded. Team names bring an extra element of competitiveness and fun.

Directions:

1. Split class into teams (preferably 4-6 students per team) and give them 1 minute to come up with a team name and to nominate a captain.

2. Explain that there will be 3 rounds and that each round will be scored separately. Write up the team names on the board and put four columns for scores.

3. Ask 6-10 questions (depending on time) for round 1 and then get teams to swap papers with another team to mark papers as the answers are given (captains make sure there is no cheating).

4. Ask for a volunteer to act as scorekeeper who then writes up the score for each team.

5. Get teams to return papers to relevant teams and repeat the process for round 2. From this point onwards team members usually become highly involved and competitiveness is increased as the progressive score totals show each team's positioning in the game.

Fun strategy #4:

Include Music in Lessons

Music has a massive effect on our young people - it is such a vital part of their lives and so big an influence that we must include it somehow. Either play it, sing it, relate lesson content to it, or just mention it to show you're on their wavelength.

Music is an instantaneous way to change the tone and mood in any classroom. You can use it to relax your students and focus their attention; to enhance creativity and boost achievement. Music can energise and bring new life to a tired group just as it can calm down a hyped-up individual. It can provide fun and a change of mind-set as well as building rapport and encouraging bonding. The right music, in the right situation, is a great team builder and a valuable aid to learning. And, of course, the opportunity to laugh at teacher's gramophone recording collection is always welcome.

Here are five ways music can be used positively in the classroom:

#1 – To help create a welcoming atmosphere

You can create the right atmosphere for your lesson by playing background music as your students enter the room. The choice of music could be linked to the theme of the lesson or could simply be 'feel-good' music as a means to relax the group.

#2 – As an aid to learning

Different types of music can be played at appropriate times during a lesson to motivate, calm, focus or relax students – different tempos and genres being more suited to a particular type of activity. A CD of TV and film theme tunes gives lots of opportunities for this: you can play 'Chariots of Fire', 'Rocky' or 'Mission impossible' at the start of lessons, Benny Hill when you want them to change activities and the 'Countdown' theme tune when you want them to answer spot questions.

Music also provides an aid to marking transitions between different lesson activities. Slowly turning the track off once all students are at their desks, gives a clear indication that the lesson is about to formally start and is far less abrasive than the usual, *"Quiet! Let's make a start!"*

A session of active learning, in which students are expected and encouraged to be moving freely around the room, could be accompanied by some lively dance music to keep the group going, while a discussion would favour a slower, less intrusive tempo. Playing this new track at a lower volume would promote a more settled atmosphere whilst still providing some cover for those who are reluctant to speak out in discussions – it can be daunting for self-conscious students to speak out during discussions. Another tune could be brought in towards the end of the discussion session to signify transition to the next activity or to bring the lesson to a close. At the end, some uplifting music would help cement positive emotions as the students file out of the room – the theme from The Great Escape, perhaps.

Baroque music has been found to stimulate right-side brain activity and aid concentration, and can be an excellent accompaniment to small group discussions and cooperative work.

#3 – To uplift and harmonise the class

Classical music can have a surprisingly positive effect on the classroom environment. Some of the most challenging students I have taught complained bitterly when I first introduced classics such as Ravel's 'Bolero' as background music to our lessons, swearing that the only sound they could possibly listen to was throbbing, hardcore rave. At first we got nowhere, predictably – they would actually sit staring at me with fingers in ears saying repeatedly, "We're not listenin', it's crap!"

Gradually, as they began to recognise tunes from various adverts and films, they became more tolerant and eventually started asking for certain pieces to be replayed. 'O Fortuna' from Carl Orff's Carmina Burana (used in the Old Spice adverts) and Delibes' 'Flower Duet' from the opera Lakme (used by British Airways) were both very popular; but so were many more. The response was actually quite amazing and, although I can provide no data to back this up, I do believe there was a much calmer atmosphere and a marked decrease in behaviour problems when these pieces of music were played at a moderate volume as background music.

#4 - As a classroom management tool

Music can act as a 'noise screen' – masking out unwanted noises and dominant voices which would otherwise distract some workers. In addition, it can provide teachers with necessary privacy when giving feedback to individual learners, or when challenging those who aren't participating as they should be.

#5 – As impromptu furniture repairs

A stack of Robbie Williams discs is ideal for propping up a wonky table leg.

Fun strategy #5:

Use Humour

One of the best ways for adding 'serotonin moments' to lessons without needing to be a comedian yourself is to include funny video clips. They can be shown as spontaneous class rewards for effort or to mark transitions between activities. Showing these short clips (just two or three minutes at most) can become a routine that students look forward to in your lessons.

YouTube provides a phenomenal amount of searchable clips to use. Here's how to convert them from YouTube and store them for use on your Whiteboard or in Powerpoint presentations.

1. You need an FLV player to view the videos once you've downloaded them. If you don't have one, typing 'free FLV player' into Google will find a selection.

2. Go to www.keepvid.com.

3. Keep the page open, open another browser window then go to www.Youtube.com.

4. When you've found the video you want to keep copy and paste the url of the video from the address space at the top of your browser. Paste this into the 'URL' box at the top of the Keepvid home page then click 'download'.

You'll then be given several download links depending on the format you want to save the video as – FLV, and probably mp4 and 3gp (for phones, ignore this one). I use FLV but by all means use mp4 if you prefer (as long as you have the player).

Important!!!

If you left-click 'download' your computer will try and save it as the default 'Get Video'. Make sure you right-click to save it to a new folder on your computer and rename it with a .flv extension or it won't work in the player. You can call the video whatever you want, but you must put '.flv' after it.

...eg Reallycoolvid.flv

5. Store the video somewhere easy to find (such as your desktop) then just drag and drop it into the FLV player. Bob's your uncle – YouTube videos in class. Lots of mirth shall be had by all. Just remember – behaviourneeds.com are not to be held responsible for the content of any videos you download, even the good ones!

Spontaneous Rewards

The most commonly used motivational strategy in schools usually involves some kind of reward programme where typically, points and pre-arranged prizes are awarded to students as they make progress along a chart or towards a points total.

I have worked in several settings where programmes like this have had a very positive, almost miraculous effect, particularly on the behaviour of students. Sadly these effects were always short-lived for a significant percentage of the students they were set up to help, and their efficacy waned with time.

No matter how elaborate or brightly painted the star chart and no matter how fantastic the prizes, some students will either become bored or frustrated with the system or the pre-arranged rewards. For many students, rewards are just not a suitable long-term strategy.

So why not?

One of the main problems with reward programmes is that they don't take into account students who lack the capacity or skills to complete a designated task or meet a required level of work – they just assume that the only reason they aren't working is because they don't want to do so. Consider a boy who is offered rewards to bring in his homework. If he lives in an acutely chaotic home where school is viewed negatively by other family members and he has never been taught even the most basic of time management skills, the reward won't help him – it won't make his family members give him support, and it won't teach him the required organisational skills to find time to sit down to do his homework.

You can find a simple example of the above in your own actions - whenever you lose a personal item, for instance. The prize or reward is finding the lost item, and if it's a particularly valuable or treasured item, the prize is great. Yet no matter how much you want your item, if you don't know how or where to find it, you're at a disadvantage - your valuable reward cannot improve your ability to locate it.

On the live version of our motivation course I use the promise of cash rewards for a series of impossible tasks to hammer this message home. Participants are offered increasingly valuable cash prizes if they manage to complete a series of puzzles. They can't do it. No matter how much they want to, no matter how much they would like to further deplete my bank account, and no matter how much I increase the potential prize money, they can't complete the task.

The reward alone is not going to motivate a student if the skills aren't present, and the reward system will ultimately prove entirely demotivating.

The second big problem with rewards is that they can divert attention from the actual task in hand which is counter to internal motivation. When the reward itself becomes the goal, the student loses interest in the task and is unlikely to feel any benefit or derive any joy from completing it for its own sake. Also, when a student becomes fixated on a reward like this, they become reliant on the view of the teacher or whoever is responsible for giving the reward – independence isn't promoted.

It's bad enough that rewards can stifle creativity and cause arguments but (in my experience) the single biggest problem from the teacher's point of view is that they only have a temporary impact. This is a huge problem in settings where rewards are perceived by staff to be the only available motivational tool. When the reward (and therefore the system) ceases to have a positive effect, the only answer lies in coming up with a variation on the same theme – another points target, a different progress chart and a new set of 'better' (in other words 'more expensive') prizes. The novelty of a 'new' system may lead to some momentary improvements but before long the problem will reoccur and yet another system will be sought.

The long term answer lies in looking deeper at the reasons behind a student's lack of motivation and then putting in place strategies and systems to address their problems. We covered this in 'Power

Strategies' – students need to be given 'opportunity to succeed' by being taught the skills they will need to complete a task.

Going back to our example above of the boy who doesn't bring his homework to school – no amount of reward (or punishment for that matter) is going to motivate him because his skills and support networks are lacking. He would be better helped by: being coached in his weak study/time management skills; being given explicit instructions in how to record and complete the homework task; and by the teacher contacting home to encourage family members to provide him with more support.

But after all this rewards themselves aren't all bad if offered wisely. Student effort should be recognised and celebrated – and rewards can be used to this end - but we can do better than to rely entirely on bribery where they are promised in advance of an achieved target, as is the case with most school reward systems. Let's look at a better way to use rewards as true motivators: offering them spontaneously as occasional surprises.

Gifts, presents and favours are always pleasing to receive but they have far more impact when they are a total surprise. One of the most effective reward systems I ever saw in operation in a school worked entirely on this basis. Unlike most other centres and special schools I'd worked in for children with behaviour difficulties, there were no sticker charts and points totals on offer here. Instead, a youth worker was assigned to take students who had shown improved effort out on a trip. The 'trip' might be a run into town; a visit to a park or sports centre; an event or show; helping out with unpacking some deliveries; or even gardening. It all depended on the level of reward the teacher felt the students deserved.

The effectiveness of this lay in the method of delivery. The youth worker would walk into the classroom (this was pre-arranged with the teacher but unbeknown to the students) and say something along the lines of: "Jonny, I hear you've been working very hard this week. I think you deserve to come out with me."

The impact this had on the other students (and Jonny of course) was quite astounding. There was no build up nor expectation on the students' part, but good effort was still positively rewarded. This approach was more about rejoicing in and celebrating achievement. The set up gave the opportunity for the teacher to say "look what happens when you work hard". It was quite a profound moment for the other students to look up and see Jonny walk out of the room.

Individual spontaneous rewards are very powerful but this approach can also be adapted for a whole group – with tremendous benefits in terms of improved social interaction between students and an enhanced community feeling. Occasional, unannounced 'just because you've all been working so hard' whole class treats such as videos (with popcorn) or bringing in cakes and soft drinks go a long way to motivating a previously disengaged group.

Here are three ways of delivering spontaneous, surprise rewards:

• Spontaneous Reward type #1: Quick individual rewards

Individual spontaneous rewards are most effective when they mean something to the student. This is one reason why it is so important to get to know students and find out their hobbies and passions. It's not as effective giving a sticker with a picture of an animal to a boy who is crazy about tractors. These individual rewards may seem small and insignificant compared to the expensive tangible prizes – record vouchers, mobile phone vouchers etc offered in school reward systems but, if chosen wisely and delivered at the right time, in the right way, they can have a great effect.

"Jonny, you kept your temper today all the way through the lesson and completed the work I set you. You can have a cup of tea at break and first choice on activities."

The following suggested spontaneous rewards can be adapted to fit any individual student's interests. Some are applicable to younger students only.

➤ Sit at the teacher's desk

➤ Time on computer

- Be in line first for lunch (can nominate a friend)

- Choose their seat for the day

- Classroom job - taking care of the class animal/s, being in charge of materials/supplies, watering plants, taking the register, operating the projector, maintaining the calendar, cleaning the board etc.

- Have lunch with the teacher

- Have lunch with the head teacher

- Join another class

- Choose the music/film

- Use special materials/equipment – special pens/paper/computer programme etc.

- Invite a visitor, speaker, entertainer from outside the school

- Show visitors round school

- Be a helper in the room with younger/less able children

- Help the secretary

- Help the librarian

- Invite a friend from another class into the room for lunch

- Take a class game home for the night

- Keep a favourite soft toy/class mascot on your desk

- Use the couch or beanbag chair

- Set up a display

- Be leader of a class game

- Get a fun worksheet from the 'fun pile'

- **Spontaneous Reward type #2: Special awards and trophies**

Awards are almost always used in classrooms in the form of certificates, but why stop there? A trophy is far more appealing – even if it is just a flimsy, plastic joke 'Oscar' – and it doesn't have to be something they take home; it's the recognition and the ceremony that counts. A very brief, simple, humorous, surprise award ceremony can take place at the end of the week or once a month/term to highlight students' progress in any given area:

- This week's 'Independent Worker' award goes to... (suggested joke trophy: Toy plastic workman figure)

- This week's 'Early Finisher' award goes to... (suggested joke trophy: Toy plastic watch)

- This week's 'Most Improved Student' is... (suggested joke trophy: Rosette, 'thumbs-up' certificate or model)

- This week's 'Mrs Mop' award for tidying the room goes to... (suggested joke trophy: some cleaning materials – a scrubbing brush?)

- This week's 'Mr Motivator' award for keeping everyone positive goes to... (suggested joke trophy: 'rah rah' cheerleader pompom or whistle)

• **Spontaneous Reward type #2: Work-related rewards**

All students like to have their work recognised – either publicly or in private.

- Allow them to show work to a younger class – as an example of the excellent work these students will be producing as they move up through the school.

- Ask the head teacher to come and look at the student's work (or send the student to the head teacher's office with their work).

- Put the work on a special 'Wall of Fame' notice board reserved for the very best work each week, or on a special display board near the school entrance.

- Make an arrangement with a local paper/free sheet publisher to feature 'excellent school work' and allow the student to send their work in for publishing.

- Compile a class/school newsletter and feature a collection of the best work in it each week/month.

- Send the work home to parents/invite parents in to view it.

- Put up a website or blog for excellent work to be displayed.

Fun strategy #7:

Multi-channel learning

Howard Gardner's 'Multiple Intelligence' theory identifies seven different ways of being clever (he has actually gone on to add two more intelligences to his model but we will keep it to seven for simplicity's sake here). While we may not necessarily agree with the intricacies of the theory – after all, who is to say that there aren't more than just nine intelligences? - there are few who would argue that the basic principle is not sound. We are all individuals, all different, and therefore must have different ways of taking in and learning new information.

During live courses we present participants with a range of activities and it is wonderful (and often quite enlightening) to see that responses to the differing types of activity produce very different responses from those involved. In one particular activity we take photos of the expressions on participants' faces and show them back on the whiteboard at the end of the activity. The message is clear for all to see – some people are totally enthralled by an activity while others are completely bemused/turned off or frustrated by the same. Adopting a 'one size fits all' approach towards teaching activities can alienate (and often annoy) as many people as it engages.

This fits perfectly with the Needs Focused Approach™ because it gives us a framework within which to meet the needs of our different students. We know that certain students do well in a maths class and yet struggle in language-based subjects. Other students show natural skill in practical subjects while at the same time struggle in academic subjects. Still others are a wizard in music or arts classes but will try to avoid sports lessons at all costs.

The thing we do know for sure is that all our students tend to perk up when we introduce a range of teaching methods. If we include AV technology and music, allow students to interact and work together in groups, encourage movement around the room and provide hands-on activities we generally find our students are motivated and eager to take part.

Each student is different and is motivated by, attracted to and skilled in different stimuli.

In effect we live in different worlds, we see the world through different eyes. If students are happy and engaged it's because we're providing activities which suit them. They each have a preferred way of doing and a favoured way of learning and if we, as teachers, provide only one style of learning activity we may well be excluding them from the entire learning process.

If we were to teach every lesson in the same way we would alienate and switch off a proportion of learners in the room, and the resulting bad behaviour and disruption would convince us that the fault lay with the students themselves. Yet if we ourselves were put in the same situation, how quick would we be to complain? Imagine for a moment that your boss or head of department restricted you in a similar fashion. How would you feel if you were ordered to write your reports in a language you could hardly speak, or were directed to present all your lesson plans pictorially?

I know this to be true because I tried it (unwittingly) for several years in my own teaching. Most of my early lessons followed the same format: I would start by introducing the topic (me talking), would lead into a demonstration (me talking, with a bit of showing), would give them instructions on how to complete a task (me still talking!) and then would let them free to do some independent work of their own, either from a book or as a practical activity (finally, a break from me talking, even if it was only to have them working from books). Not surprisingly, it wasn't uncommon for me to have mutiny on my hands.

If we want them to be motivated we have to provide activities and tasks which appeal to them – activities they can get their teeth into and derive satisfaction from. There is an old saying which has always stuck in my mind – 'if you want them to do good work, give them good work to do' and one way of making sure we are giving them work which has a good chance of appealing to them is to incorporate Gardner's theory of Multiple Learning Intelligences and provide a range and variety of tasks.

Questions to ask yourself when planning a lesson using multiple learning intelligences:

Logical/mathematical - could I include more logical/critical thinking, problem-solving or strategy games?

Kinesthetic – could I include more movement/tactile activities? What practical tasks can I include?

Spatial – could I present information in the form of a jigsaw or other image-based format?

Musical – could I present information over a rhythm or backing track? Could students translate content into a musical form?

Linguistic – Can I present this information as a discussion or debate?

Interpersonal – Which cooperative learning format can I use to present this information?

Intrapersonal – Which tasks can I give to students who prefer to work alone?

In the Multiple Intelligences Reminder, there is a selection of possible learning activities to adapt lesson content so that it encompasses these seven different learning channels.

Make work relevant to them

Students respond most positively in lessons when tasks and challenges are connected to what they know in the real world so we have to introduce new topics and information to them in a way that is relevant to them if we want them to be interested.

Let me give you an example from my own teaching experience to illustrate how this might be done.

I used to teach Shakespeare to teenage boys who had been excluded from mainstream school. Let's get it clear that these boys seldom spoke in recognisable, grammatically correct sentences. Monosyllabic grunts were the chosen mode of expression, so you can probably imagine what they thought of Shakespeare.

The first year I struggled to find suitable resources to engage them. Text books that claimed to be packed with engaging activities for low ability, disengaged students proved to be of little use. The government frameworks which provided very prescriptive three-part lessons (written by highly paid consultants) were even less useful. After three or four lessons the mere mention of the word 'Shakespeare' set these boys into a rage threatening to literally rip the room apart if I tried to inflict any more on them.

So how does a teacher introduce a writer such as Shakespeare, so far removed from modern life, to a group of 15-year-old boys? How does one get them to identify with him and see him as having something to offer, so that they might be interested enough to at least listen to part of a play... you know, just in case he's actually any good?

My new cohort of students came to my lessons already hating Shakespeare. They hated the language (largely because they couldn't understand it) and other kids in school who'd already had to endure him told them that the Shakespeare lessons were, in a word, 'crap'. I was beaten before the lesson had started. They'd already made up their minds that S.h.a.k.e.s.p.e.a.r.e spelled 'shit'.

Yet in the late 1500s and early 1600s (long before the first 15-year-old boys stalked the earth) Shakespeare wrote plays which captured hearts and minds. His plays were tremendously entertaining and the public flocked to see them. He was the Quentin Tarantino of his day (though probably a better actor). So that's how I introduced him to the class. I didn't even mention the name at first. Instead we talked about films the students had all watched. Horror films, comedies, and gangster films such as Reservoir Dogs got them talking. We talked about the emotions they evoked and why they found them so entertaining.

I asked them what they would do without television and cinema. What entertainment was on offer before this technology became such a part of our lives? Most of them had heard of these buildings called theatres, but probably couldn't have told one apart from a supermarket, and none had actually been inside one. So I organised a trip. They loved it. They wanted to know more about this interactive, wonderful form of entertainment. And from that point on they had an interest in William Shakespeare where previously there had been ignorance, fear and loathing.

Shakespeare was made interesting to these boys over a series of lessons but the key was first getting them to see that the entertainment they loved was the very same entertainment that was loved hundreds of years ago – it was made relevant to them. Shakespeare wrote comedies, dramas and bloody tragedies which were adored by his fans – the film-goers of yesteryear. Once the students could see that there were parallels between the entertainment back then and the blockbusters of today, they were interested to learn more.

If we can show students new ideas through something they already enjoy outside school, they will be more receptive to those new ideas. Making better connections between the work and your students' lives is easier when you actually know what's going on in their lives; but even without detailed knowledge of each student's interests, likes and dislikes etc, you can still tailor lesson tasks to youth culture and real life in general - something which is relevant to all of them.

Here are some more ways of making work relevant to your students:

i) Link to current real-world problems

The integration of current social context into a subject encourages students to move away from seeing the subject as far removed from their lives. Can you start the lesson by talking about a recent news item or a relevant real-life issue that this particular age-group are interested in or affected by?

ii) Link to their environment

By taking the curriculum out into the real world and showing how knowledge can be used in their own habitat we give them immediate relevance. Can you start the lesson by linking content to a photograph of their town centre, a newspaper article about their neighbourhood, a news video about a local event or area or even by taking them out into the environment?

iii) Link to their interests

In our section on 'Belonging' we highlighted the importance of discovering and getting to know your students' interests and hobbies. Linking content to students' interests is one of the best ways for them to see the importance of a topic but even in the absence of detailed personal information about each student, there are common areas which will be of interest to most: sport, fashion/image, celebrities, music, TV.

iv) Link to age-appropriate real-life issues

Adolescence, for example, is a very troubling time for most teenagers with serious issues which they find confusing and difficult. When information is linked to issues which students may be experiencing such as gangs/gang culture, drugs, confidence, self esteem, they can empathise and are therefore able to see the relevance in what is being presented.

v) Use metaphors and analogies

Metaphors and analogies are one of the very best ways of making new concepts relevant to students because they draw parallels between the new information and previously-known, commonplace or everyday objects, happenings or actions.

I use metaphors and analogies A LOT in my teaching to describe processes, actions, concepts, in fact virtually anything, because they give students an easy way to grasp and understand new material. You could say it's like turning a light on for them or providing them with a map. And there's an easy way to come up with a metaphor for virtually anything you're teaching. Just ask yourself a simple question: "What is it like?" and pick the answer which you feel would be most relevant to your students.

For example, diffusion – the spread of particles from regions of higher concentration to regions of lower concentration - is a difficult concept to explain to students so let's ask the question: *"What's it like?"*

a) It's like watching people travelling down a tightly packed escalator and then all spreading out in different directions when they get to the bottom.

b) It's like watching the smoke from a bonfire spread out.

c) It's like hearing a student breaking wind at the back of the class and then watching the succession of other class members clutching their noses as the chemical weapon spreads through the room.

Any one of those analogies could be used to describe the process of 'diffusion' in a way that students who had no concept of the process could relate to it. For some reason, most of my students found analogy 'c' easiest to relate to.

vi) Ask the right sort of questions

I used to start the majority of my lessons with a question relating to the topic focus. For example, if I was doing a lesson on the circulatory system, my opening question might be: *"How many of you can explain what a blood vessel is?"*

A few students would be eager to answer me and their hands would shoot up so I thought I was doing the right thing. I had some participation after all. But for every hand that went up there were ten more that didn't. A significant proportion of the students simply weren't taking part. And if they are not taking part, as we well know, they soon start to misbehave.

Let's face it, it was a dull question. No matter how passionately it is delivered that type of question isn't likely to generate much involvement from the group. Questions like this rely on volunteers, and if you rely on volunteers you are immediately switching your attention and lesson focus towards those students who already want to learn.

That makes it far too easy for those who aren't motivated to learn to simply sit and watch, perhaps pretending to listen. Why should they bother taking part? They find the subject dull and they either don't know the answer to the question or just don't want to answer. Maybe they are afraid of looking 'swotty' in front of their peers; maybe they don't want to risk the embarrassment of getting it wrong (remember the demotivators we mentioned?). It's easier just to sit and watch. Or sit and fiddle. Or walk out.

If you want to get the non-volunteers involved you've got to have a question that they can relate to, something that relates to their interests or is at least relevant to their lives and experiences. Why would they even care how blood gets round the body unless the question is relevant to them? See if you can spot the difference between the following styles of question:

A) Who can tell me how blood gets round the body?

B) Who knows what a blood vessel is?

C) Can anyone tell me what a blood capillary is?

D) When did you last cut your finger badly?

A) Give me five differences between Macbeth's character before and after he kills Duncan.

B) How does Macbeth change after he kills Duncan?

C) What words would you use to describe Macbeth at the start of the play?

D) When was the last time you did something really terrible that you later regretted?

Can you see why 'D' in both cases would be far more likely to get them listening and switched on? Those questions hook them by giving them opportunity to think about events that are relevant to them or have had a direct effect on them.

Okay, that's the type of question that will 'hook' your students, but we then need to follow up with further questions to get them 'into' the lesson content. The complete set of questions you put to them might look something like this:

• When did you last cut your finger badly?

• How long did it bleed for?

• How did you stop the bleeding?

• Do you think it would it have stopped if you had just left it?

• Where does the blood come from and how does it get to the cut?

• ...leading nicely to a discussion on capillaries and blood vessels – the lesson topic.

vii) Use case studies

Case studies can be a description of a situation or an excerpt of dialogue from a situation. By choosing situations which are applicable to student life, almost any lesson topic can be presented in the form of a case study. Here's a sample case study from one of our Classroom Management courses to show how a subject is taught by presenting a situation which students can relate to:

Case Study 3: Needs Focused Classroom Management Home Study Course

Teacher: Gestures to John to take his headphones off?

John: [No response]

Teacher: [Moves closer, smiling and mimes taking the headphones off] Hey John, could you remove the earphones please?

John: Eh?

Teacher: The earphones – take them off please.

John: What for?

Teacher: Because I'm talking to the group. For the second time, take off the headphones and put them away.

John: I'm fine, I can hear.

Teacher: (Very calmly) John, I'm asking you for the third and final time; take off your headphones and put them away please. [moves away from John]

John: I can hear.

Teacher: (Very calmly) OK John, you know the rules; go to time out.

In this version of the same situation from Case Study 1 the teacher uses the '3 requests' technique to give John a clear, calm warning.

a) What other consequence/s could be used instead of Time Out?

b) What else could the teacher have said or done to make John reflect on his behaviour and consider his next move more sensibly?

c) What could/should the teacher do if John refused to leave the room?

Suggested questions for case studies:

• What would you do in this situation?

• How does this relate to...... ?

• If you were (the victim/shopkeeper/student/etc) what would you do?

• What five mistakes did the person make in this situation?

• What five things did the person do right in this situation?

• Give three examples of ...... from the above case study

Assignment 4:

1) Intrigue: Invite attention and promote curiosity:

Try to start at least one lesson a week with something intriguing. Make changes to normal routines and give students nice surprises as highlighted in Fun Strategy #1.

2) Role Play & Drama:

Provide the suggested drama and role play opportunities in lessons – even if only as five-minute fill-ins or energisers.

3) Active Learning:

Start a file or folder of starter activities, plenaries, teach-backs, mini-reviews, energisers and classroom games. Try to include some of these in every lesson.

4) Music:

Start a collection of suitable music to use in lessons and use selected tunes to accompany lesson activities and transitions.

5) Humour:

Start a collection of funny videos using YouTube and use them in lessons for occasional 'serotonin moments'.

6) Spontaneous Rewards:

Start a collection of fun trophies and recognise individual and group effort with occasional unplanned, surprise rewards.

7) Multi-Channel Learning:

Try to include activities and tasks which appeal to a variety of learning styles using the Multiple Intelligence Teaching Strategies reminder.

8) Relevancy:

Whenever possible, use the strategies outlined to make new content relevant to student life.

Bonus Section: Dealing With Motivation Problems

We've looked at ways to minimise demotivating factors and promote intrinsic motivation in students – the Needs-Focused preventive strategies. This next section covers a range of ways to respond to some of the problems you'll face in a classroom environment populated by unmotivated students. It's a fact of any teacher's life, no matter how fluffy and positive you've made your classroom, no matter how many preventive strategies you're using - kids are kids; there will be problems! These strategies may be helpful when the problems occur.

Before we get properly started on the responses, I want to mention a couple of important points. Firstly, this little selection of scripts and strategies does not represent the last word on behaviour management. I don't profess to have all the answers - not by a long piece of chalk - and I'm sure there are some points I make which fly in the faces of psychological/biological/educational theory.

Here's something to think about though... did you know that many parenting books are written by 'experts' who've never even been a parent, and many behaviour management books are written by academics who haven't set foot in a classroom since they were students themselves? I'm a practical man, not a theorist. What makes me so confident about these common sense strategies is that I know through real, practical experience in the classroom that they work. I have used these ideas in some very challenging settings with some equally challenging (and vulnerable) students and they worked for me. They helped me not only to survive but to succeed; they helped my students and they helped me. So I don't really care what theorists say. The proof of the pudding, so they say, is in the eating - and when you get it right it tastes just fine.

However, you'll find that these strategies work much, much better if they are used within a framework in which the preventive strategies to satisfy Belonging, Power and Fun are already firmly in place. Remember at the start of all this we said that any attempt to motivate students will only work properly if the dreaded demotivators are first reduced? Well, that's the purpose of the preventive strategies. Get those set up first and you'll find these responses having much more impact.

Now, before we go through the scenario-specific responses there are two fundamentals which will certainly have relevance regardless of the particular problem you're dealing with...

1. Always try to find the reason for the problem.

There's a reason for everything (I'm reminded of that fact every time I go to the bank and remember why I'm broke – it's because I spend too much). There is always a reason why a student doesn't want to start work. There's always a reason why they shout out. There's always a reason why they hit each other. Whatever the problem, there's a reason why it's happening.

Telling him to 'get on with his work' is a typical stock response when Jonny is messing around but it doesn't address the underlying reasons he's off task and therefore doesn't usually work – certainly not for long. He might get his head down while you stand over him but as soon as your back his turned Jonny will revert to unscrewing the table leg unless the underlying issue has been addressed – in this case that the table leg is infinitely more interesting than the worksheet you've given him!

If you're faced with students who flatly refuse to get started, are constantly chatting, are totally uninterested in the exciting task put before them or turn up to class two days late, it's best to try and find the reason why this might be happening before trying to stop it happening again.

The problem could be any of the de-motivators we mentioned early on in this resource pack (fear, boredom etc). But why bother second guessing? The only way to find out for sure what is behind their reluctance to take part is to ask them. This is obviously best done out of earshot of other students and in a non-threatening manner and once a trusting, mutually respectful teacher/student relationship has been established.

2. Be consistent.

All students – those you are dealing with, as well as those watching you deal with them, need to see you being consistent. They need to know that you will deal with anyone who is not doing as they should be every time they are not doing it. After all, if any student is witnessed by others to be 'getting away with it', you can bet your life that other students will be encouraged to try getting away with it too. Then you've got real problems.

An easy way to remember it is this: **If you allow it, you encourage it.**

Letting Vanessa wear her headphones (because she has an awful temper and really kicks off when challenged) sends a clear signal to her and others – she will wear them again, as will the six others who saw her get away with it. When you bend the rules for one, you create a rod for your own back.

In every classroom situation there are going to be students who push boundaries too far no matter how positive and student-centred you are. Some won't respect a teacher who is too 'nice.' Some are intent on ruining a lesson no matter how engaging and exciting the tasks. Some think any teacher who doesn't have tattoos is a push-over. These are all reasons why a system of stepped consequences, consistently applied, is essential.

Hopefully the setting you're working in will have a behaviour policy in place and will provide you with a nice selection of shiny consequences for you to take down off the shelf and use in response to each and every behaviour problem which occurs. But just remember, it's the way you apply these consequences which affects their success – you have to be consistent. You can't use them one day and not the next, can't apply them to one student and not the next, or apply them with a patronising sneer to one student and an apologetic wince to another. You must do what you say you're going to do – every time.

If your rule on not finishing work in class is that students have to return at break or stay behind after school for ten minutes to finish it - then it must happen. And remember, if you don't chase up the 'no-shows' then you may as well not bother with having the rule in the first place. Yes, chasing up these 'detention dodgers' will be time consuming, but only in the short term. It's a case of 'short term pain for long term gain'. Being consistent means keeping detailed records every time they miss a scheduled meeting or detention too. It might mean liaising with form tutors and heads of year. It might mean making countless phone calls home or even embarking on home visits. But all this leg work builds your reputation as indomitable and once they get the fact that you don't give in, that you follow up every time - they will start to be tamed and you will start to save time. You'll no longer have to constantly repeat your instructions. You'll be the teacher who walks in a room and gets immediate respect and compliance from the rowdiest group. Short term pain, long term gain.

Oh, nearly forgot, while we're on the subject of consequences, don't get emotional when giving them either. A calm, matter-of-fact approach is far more effective than shrieking and wailing – no matter how much eye rolling, muttering, complaining and swearing they try. Keep the emotional outbursts for the times they have done something right. If you have a penchant for standing on the table shouting, do it when Jonny has finished his first essay – by way of celebration.

Finally, don't get drawn into their attempts to start an argument; this will not only give them the reaction they are trying to provoke (making you appear weak in the process), you will also run the risk of the situation escalating to a much more serious incident. Once they get you started, they don't want to stop.

On my live training courses I always deal with consequences last because I want to hammer home the clear message that there are a multitude of effective preventive strategies to encourage students to stay on the right tracks before needing to resort to sanctioning: focusing on building positive relationships; using sincere praise as often as possible; making sure instructions and directions are explicit;

getting parents involved; setting up buddy schemes; having student meetings; integrating cooperative group work; putting humour in lessons; giving them responsibilities, to name just a few.

The reason I labour this message is not because I'm against sanctioning but because there is a danger people will rely on consequences as the only available behaviour response. Doing so can create a very punitive, oppressive atmosphere which causes more problems than it solves. We need consequences to enforce boundaries and kids need boundaries in order to feel secure – but like any tool they should be used properly, and not relied upon as an easy way out.

So those two points – trying to find the reason for the behaviour and having a hierarchy of consistently applied consequences on hand - are necessary for most problems we come across. Let's look now at the specific responses...

Problem #1:

No interest in the lesson

A student who has no interest in lessons and a negative attitude towards anything you say and do can have a terrible impact on the rest of the class. But what you must remember is that this student probably wants to succeed – most do deep down, it's just that he has all but given up due to a succession of failures, discouragement and low self image. It may take time to reach this student and help him see life (or at least your lessons) differently but there are definitely steps to take which will help turn the situation round more quickly.

1. Look to praise anything and everything you can - sincerely.
Students with a very low self image may be uncomfortable receiving praise in front of others so start off by using written praise. Send notes home, leave post-it notes or written comments in their books, send them cards or typed letters on school-headed paper stating how pleased you are with their efforts, and include anything positive you have heard from another teacher. This kid needs to know he has

potential and that somebody is taking the time to notice. Sincere, heartfelt praise is one of the most powerful tools you possess and as long as you come from the position of wanting to help this student (as opposed to just using a 'suitable behaviour intervention to try and get them to listen to you') he will respond.

2. Do some research. Speak to other teachers, their form tutor or head of year to find out if there are any underlying issues you should be aware of. A tutor who has a good relationship with a particularly hard to reach student can give you 'insider tips' to connect with this student as well as notify you of any 'hot issues' to avoid.

3. Schedule a 1:1 meeting with the student. Purpose: to ask why they are so uninterested, ask their advice on making lessons more engaging for them and help them to see the relevance of what they are being asked to do.

If you feel they are unlikely to turn up for a 1:1 meeting, don't worry - you can increase the chances by proposing it at the right time. There's no point telling them you want to see them in your office when they're in their 'I hate you and your lessons' mood; they won't be interested. Wait, instead, for a time when they are going to be more receptive. A good time is when you've caught them doing something well, when you've praised them for a job well done, when you've just complimented them on their new hair style/shoes/grade/tattoo or when you've seen them doing something they're good at and enjoy. You can use that time as a reference point to connect with them and start the conversation.

For example, if they play football on the school team, go and watch the game. They'll see you on the side line and will respect you for that. Next time you see them you can mention the game and talk about the goal they scored or their part in the brilliant teamwork. Now they're listening and they know that you want to help them. This would be a better time to suggest the meeting.

4. Change seating. Put them with a partner or other group members who will encourage them and help them.

5. Put them in a diverse (mixed ability) learning team and give them a definite role or responsibility. To get them involved this role should play to their strengths or abilities. For example if they are good at drawing let them be in charge of graphics or illustrations. If they have trouble sitting still let them be a 'runner' in charge of collating materials, equipment and resources.

6. Involve parents/carers. Having parents on board is a big advantage dealing with any student problems – the more we can present a united front between school and home, the better. The problem, as we all know, is that some parents just don't seem interested.

It's a huge problem when parents and other family members have deeply entrenched negative experiences of school going back through several generations - they are apprehensive about dealing with teachers. If they themselves failed at school and consequently aren't living the life of their dreams, it's not surprising that they lack the faith in education we expect and need them to have. Added to that, if their child has been a source of constant distress at school, any contact these parents have had with staff at the school is likely to have been negative. They'll have been told when he has been missing school, when he's repeatedly failed to hand in homework, when he's been in a fight and when he's been abusive to a member of staff.

A good way, if not the only way, to start to get these parents on side is to change their expectation that every communication from school will be a negative one. The more time you spend connecting with them through regular positive contact, the more they will get used to the idea that a call from school doesn't automatically ruin their day.

A 30-second update a couple of times a week – "Hi Maureen, just a quickie to let you know he's been great this week; homework was in on time and he managed to keep it together in maths again." – goes a long way towards doing this. And despite what anyone says, I've witnessed enough 'hard' fathers and 'rough' mothers breaking down in tears in my office when given news of a son or daughter's good progress to believe that this is worth doing.

7. Give them a taste of success. Students who are reluctant to take part probably see no value in learning because they never feel they've learned anything. Here's a practical way to give them a sense of accomplishment and leave your lesson feeling they've actually had some success. When they leave feeling like that, they will return in a more positive frame of mind.

1. Ask them a question at the start of the lesson related to the lesson content. (They will probably refuse to answer but that's okay – it's probably their fear of looking 'too clever' or fear of making a fool of themselves).

2. Take the pressure off them by offering them to nominate a friend who can help them answer the question/answer it for them. (This is easy for them to do – but the key is that they will see themselves as being INVOLVED in the answering process).

3. Ask them to paraphrase what their friend said so that they answer the question themselves.

4. Later in the lesson when other students are involved in independent study coach the student further by getting them to answer the question for you again on a 1:1 basis. Encourage them to break the answer down into clear steps so that they are totally sure of the process. Offer a little extra 'in-depth' information to add to their answer and ask them once more to show off their new knowledge and tell you 'all they know' about the subject. Congratulate them and tell them you will be asking them at the end of the lesson to repeat their answer to help the other students remember (the extra 'in-depth' knowledge you've given them will give them the opportunity to shine if they wish).

5. At the end of the lesson let them leave on a high by answering the question again as part of your plenary session.

6. Get them to answer the question next lesson as part of your starter.

Remember that you don't need to limit this strategy to just one student during a lesson. You can feasibly have four or five students all leaving class feeling that they've actually learned something.

Problem #2:

Low-level disruption

This sort of disruption can be like water torture to the teacher, that incessant symphony of pencil tapping, silly noises, poking, bogey-flicking, giggling, inappropriate farting (although I'm struggling to think of a time when that's appropriate), paper-passing, ruler-slapping, desk shoving, hair-pulling, and general fidgeting.

Kids will be kids, and in themselves many of the above are all fairly harmless activities (though those involving bodily functions can be hard to stomach, and hair-pulling can really hurt). Taken collectively they are incredibly wearing and can make your life hell.

There are as many ways of dealing with low level disruption as there are types of disruption – from use of humour to thumb screws – but I'm going to give you a stepped script which you may find handy because it can be used to address virtually any type of low-level interruption when it has finally got to the point where you can't take it any more...

1. State what they are doing, and what you want them to do instead. The first thing to do is point out very clearly what they are doing wrong. It's surprising the effect this can have on them – sometimes they might not be aware how annoying their behaviour is for other people in the room until it is spelled out to them. In terms of what you want them to do you need to make their choices as simple as possible and leave no room for misunderstanding. You also need to explain why they should do what you're asking – ie, tell them what will happen if they don't follow your instructions. By doing this you show that you're not just getting on their backs just for the sake of it – there are reasons for your actions. This of course, gives them fewer excuses to complain or argue.

"John you're not doing your work and you're putting everyone off with that tapping. You need to pick your pen up and finish your target so that you don't have to get it finished in your own time."

If they don't immediately start doing as you've asked or if they answer you with a promise to do it soon, you should move on to stage 2. A promise that they will do as you ask 'in a minute' or 'later' is their way of trying to control the situation – so treat it as if they have ignored you and move to stage 2.

2. Explain exactly what will happen to them if they continue disrupting the lesson or ignoring you. Tell them very clearly what the sanction will be if they continue - clearly and without fuss or emotion. Avoid humour too – by now they have crossed the line.

"If you don't manage to get the work that I've set for you finished, you will end up losing 5 minutes of break."

"If you don't stop throwing the bits of eraser you'll have to spend your break clearing the floor."

3. Now you need to give them time to think about your instruction. Immediately follow on by giving them a time limit and then back off, walk away and give them some space. Allow them to save face. It's hard for them to jump to attention and do what you want when you're standing over them, particularly if their friends are watching (and of course you know they are).

"I'm going to give you thirty seconds to do as I've asked."

"I'll be back in less than a minute and I expect to see it done."

It's all about telling them exactly where the boundary is and exactly what they have to do to get back on the right path. By backing off – walking to another part of the room or going to help another student - you're giving them a chance to back down without losing face; you're giving them an escape route. A child backed into a corner finds it difficult to back down in front of their classmates if you're standing over them and will react accordingly – usually with more defiance. By walking away you take the pressure off.

4. If they do as you've asked, acknowledge it. A few words is all that's needed to let them know they did the right thing and to encourage them to do it in future. It's a big step they've just taken. Don't lecture them about how they should follow instructions faster next time; just give them a sincere smile and some quiet private praise.

Younger students can be rewarded more formally – perhaps by giving them a sticker or a certificate for meeting the behaviour target 'Follow teacher's instructions'.

5. If they choose not to follow your instructions then you simply give them their consequence:

"Ok you've chosen to carry on doing...... That's fine. You'll be staying in at break for 5 minutes. Now get on with your work so that you don't lose any more of your time."

6. If the consequence has little or no effect. If the behaviour resumes after a few minutes respite, repeat the procedure with a tougher consequence this time: the next in your hierarchy. This is why you should always start off with a small consequence. If you wheel out your big guns straight away – threatening to take away their entire break instead of just five minutes - you have no reserves if they continue to misbehave.

"John, if you don't stop talking I'm going to keep you behind for five minutes at break."

"You've already lost 5 minutes of your break, if you don't want to lose another 5 minutes you need to pick up the rubber you just threw."

"John, that's your whole break gone, I warned you. Unless you want me to keep you behind after school I suggest you settle down and get the work finished."

Problem #3:

Refusal to take part/start work

When you're trying to encourage less than enthusiastic students to start work it's important to make it easy for them to do so.

On my travels as a 1:1 coach in classrooms I've watched teachers heaping attention and praise on the 'good' students whilst making it quite obvious that they don't actually like the more challenging students - and then they wonder why these students don't want to get involved. I have to point out to the teacher in question that they're giving the clear message (however unintentionally) that they would rather these 'difficult' students weren't in the room. Their body language, facial expressions and attitudes scream "I don't like you. I find you threatening/worthless/smelly (insert negative adjective of choice)".

Kids, like all of us, can read body language. They notice facial expressions and they sense the attitude and general feelings we have towards them. They will never join in if they feel they aren't wanted; the hurdle is just too big for them. If I can be allowed to link back to psychological needs - it's fairly obvious that they are going to gain a greater sense of empowerment by playing up or opting out than by getting involved in something where they feel unwelcome and unappreciated.

From a practical point of view we can try the following additional strategies to encourage reluctant students to get started:

1. Targets. Targets are so important for re-engaging a student who is just starting to waver. Let's say Jonny is messing around, off-task, being mildly disruptive. It may well be that he's just not clear about what he's supposed to be doing, he may be confused, he may have misheard or he may just be a bit bored. An excellent tip for getting him back on-task is to define a very clear work target for him to achieve, and a set time in which to do so.

"Jonny, this is your target – I want you to get to number 6 by half past ten." (This is said very quietly so as not to disrupt the pace of the lesson or raise the attention of other students).

Giving targets gives very clear instructions as to how to succeed in your lesson. Boys in particular work much better when they know exactly what is expected of them and some students can only cope with small chunks of work at a time. Target setting is perfect for achieving both these aims and can have a magical calming effect on most students who are refusing to get started.

I used this method with all my classes when I was teaching. Once I'd given them their task I would go round and put a pencil mark where I expected each of them to get to in a set time:

"By ten past 11 Sarah you need to have completed the work to this mark – that's your target."

It's best to do this quietly because some students are self conscious about having smaller targets than others, and quarrels can result if different students are seen to be given higher or lower targets than their peers. Once you've done this a few times they get used to it and accept their individual targets quite happily. In fact, most lessons I'd have students actually asking me to give them a target!

There are often reluctant workers who are, in fact, very capable and you may have to   explain to these students that you'll be giving them a bigger target (more work) than anyone else. If you did this without explanation an uproar would result, but by taking them to one side before the lesson and quietly playing to their need to be noticed you can very effectively put them in a productive mood before they've even seen the task.

"Shaun, I'm going to set you a high target today because I know you can excel at this. I wouldn't be doing my job right if I didn't give you the chance to show me what you can do. Okay?"

2. Limited Choices. It is more pleasing to be given a choice than to be cornered into making a decision, or forced to do something, which is why this is such an effective way to get students working. Limited choices are questions we give to students to 'sweeten' our instructions. It is far less hostile and therefore invites fewer arguments.

"Do you want to use a blue pen or a black pen to do the work?"

"Do you want me or Jason to help you do the work?"

"Do you want to sit here or over there to finish the work?"

"Do you want to try this or that question first?"

"Do you want to finish the work now like everyone else or do you want to give up your break and finish it then?"

These limited choices still convey the message 'you're going to do the work' but because they allow a certain amount of autonomy they are easier to swallow. Nobody likes being told what to do and when you've already made up your mind that you don't want to take part, being given orders from the teacher can be too much to accept and is likely to provoke arguments. Giving them limited choices gives some control back to them; being able to make a choice for themselves, however small or controlled that choice is, often allows them to save face.

3. Get them interested with a starter activity

• Video clip

• Puzzle

• Set of questions on last lesson's key points

• Cloze exercise

• A ranking or ordering exercise. "Put these words/objects/pictures in order from easiest to hardest/best to worst/weakest to strongest/least important to most important etc." For some reason, reluctant students seem to really enjoy this type of exercise.

• Any kind of challenge: "You've got five minutes to think of as many…. as you can. Write them down and share them with your partner. Pick your best ten between the two of you and then we'll all share."

4. Change seating:

"You can work at the front until you've got down to question 5 and then I'll let you move back to your usual seat."

5. Partner them with a student who can help them.

6. Alter the work: Speak to them in private to find out what they are struggling with. Whenever possible remind them of past successes and capabilities or start by offering them support. They are more likely to listen when you start with something positive rather than nagging.

7. Have stepped consequences in place:

"What are you supposed to be doing? What happens if you don't do it? Is that what you want? What are you going to choose?"

Problem #4:

Interrupting/chatting

A lesson doesn't necessarily have to be totally silent in order to be a success but if noise levels get to the point where they are affecting others, it's time to take charge...

1. Assess your delivery. Have you been talking too long? Almost all my early lessons consisted of a relatively long didactic introduction. I meant well because I wanted to ensure everyone knew what they were doing, but students' attention spans are much shorter than ours and it's unrealistic to expect them to sit in silence for any more than five minutes at a time.

Have you used intrigue to get their attention? Have you chopped the work up into focused, bite-sized sections? Have you included breaks and humorous energisers? Is the work achievable? Have you made it relevant to them? Have you tried to include topics they find interesting? Are you playing background music and changing the tune during transitions? Are you using active learning strategies to keep them engaged and on-task?

If they are chatting excessively it's because the work and/or your delivery hasn't captured them.

2. Give no attention to those shouting. Instead, make positive statements about the behaviour you want to see:

"Thank you for your responses – I'll answer anyone who puts their hand up without calling out."

"Thanks to people on this table for raising your hands."

3. Try to deal with the problem positively (there's more chance they will listen when we start by saying something positive):

"You have a right to be listened to but you need to talk at the right time."

"You're a good talker, let's hear what you have to say about the work."

"You have a great speaking voice – we should use that – you can read the next chapter."

4. Alter seating. Split the group into diverse (mixed ability) groups to encourage peer support or partner the offending student with someone who can help keep them on task. Use choices to introduce the idea that a seating change is likely to happen if they continue talking.

"Paul you can either carry on sitting where you are and work without talking or you'll have to move to this chair at the front and work there without talking. The choice is yours."

5. Praise small steps. Either verbally or with a written note placed on their work:

"Thank you, you've been quiet for the last ten minutes – keep it up. Let's set a timer and see if you can get to the next ten minutes."

6. Have a no-nonsense approach. Start with non-verbal gestures; hold your arm out, palm facing them as a 'stop' signal. If they continue, walk into their territory whilst talking (remember, keep the lesson flowing); then put your hand on their desk or on their book to let them know you don't approve of them interrupting you. If they carry on, don't get wound up, just tell them you're bored and that their talking is preventing other people from learning. Then move on to stepped consequences as outlined above.

Problem #5:

Poor attitude and underachieving

Students who are underachieving need as much support and guidance as possible, but the amount of time you give to them has to be balanced against your responsibility to teach the other students in the group. This is where regular, frequent 1:1 meetings are so important and useful. They can help prevent situations getting progressively worse for a student to the point where emergency, highly concentrated intervention and support is necessary.

Initiating 1:1 meetings at the start of term provides opportunity to build bonds with students so that they feel happier talking about difficult situations as they arise and can be encouraged to set themselves targets and goals. It's much more effective than waiting until they reach crisis point and then trying to get them to open up and respond to help.

If you haven't had the chance to set up such meetings or are dealing with a student who hasn't responded to that strategy here are a couple of additional interventions to try:

1. Allocate a buddy

Choose a student who is doing well in class and is managing to complete work to a reasonable standard yet is well respected among peers. Set up a meeting between the two on the premise that this is to help the underachieving student get over a difficult hurdle. Provide the buddy with resources and guidance to help the student.

2. Get the parents/carers on board

Getting in touch with parents is usually a last resort for some teachers - and when treated as such rarely brings about the positive change it is capable of doing. When parents are only contacted on rare occasions, to complain about their child's behaviour, it's little wonder that they aren't very supportive.

If instead parents are contacted on a regular basis as part of a preventive approach with short updates of progress being made, they are far more likely to be strong allies when requested to help with a student who is underachieving.

Problem #6:

Poor punctuality

Having them wander in late is a common problem, particularly with older students, but much can be done to prevent it by having clear, consistent rules on punctuality backed up by cast-iron consequences. Students need to know exactly what will happen if they are late and that you will apply the consequences every time, regardless of the excuse. Don't forget the positive approach though - occasionally make a point of rewarding students when they are on time!

A tendency to be avoided is to give too much attention to those who wander in to the classroom ten minutes late with the tell-tale 'partying all night' sunken eyes and matching attitude. The natural reaction is to yell at them for their rudeness but this can give them the reaction the reaction they want and the status they enjoy. Instead, concentrate efforts on the rest of your students who did make it to class on time (even if they are currently dozing happily at the back).

Latecomers should never be allowed to disrupt your lesson so here's a step-by-step plan for dealing with them...

1. Give them as little attention as possible. Calmly, and without fuss, take their name (assuming you don't already know it) and confirm that they are late:

"John, you're ten minutes late...."

2. Direct them to their seat. Quickly direct them to a seat and give them something to occupy them – they could watch the remainder of an explanation/demonstration or get on with a worksheet or written task while you concentrate on the other learners. Don't start asking them why they're late at this stage.

"...Sit there please and get on with (insert task), you can explain why you're late after the lesson."

3. Praise those who are working. Take the focus off the latecomer by giving attention to those who are doing the right thing

"Excellent work you two, nice to see you getting on with that."

4. Address latecomers separately once other students are settled. Once the majority of the students are working the next step is to get the latecomer/s engaged properly in the lesson task. This can be done by either gathering them as one group and giving them the full demonstration/lesson introduction again or (better) pair them up with other students who can teach them or explain the task to them.

5. Follow up with latecomers at the end of the lesson. Students who were on time can, if feasible and appropriate, be given a slightly early finish to enable you to follow up for no more than two minutes with those who were late (see 'The Two-Minute Follow-Up' below). Get latecomers to fill in a form stating the time they arrived and reason for lateness. This provides you with valuable proof to send home if the problem continues.

The Two Minute Follow Up

The two minute follow-up takes place at the end of the lesson. This is the time you keep behind any student who has caused a problem during the lesson – those who have forgotten to bring equipment, those who were late, making silly comments etc.

If you have too many students to speak to during the two minutes, or you feel you need more than two minutes, tell them they must come back and see you at the start of break. Of course, if the lesson falls just before break you have the luxury of being able to keep them for slightly longer than two minutes without worrying about disrupting the next lesson. Tell them that if they don't turn up at the allotted time, the result will be an after-school Ten Minute Detention.

The follow up is not a time to lecture and rant at students. It is merely an opportunity to acknowledge that there has been a problem. They still get the message that their behaviour must change, but they are far more likely to do so when they are not focused on feelings of anger and retribution.

Things to say to students during a follow-up:

i) Introduce the reason they are with you.

"I don't want to be on your case all the time so what can we do to stop this happening in future?"

"I want you to have a chance at succeeding here so shall we try and work out some ways we can work well together without these recurring problems?"

ii) Tackle the issue

When establishing what they did wrong avoiding asking them 'why' they did it. The word 'why' is very confrontational and puts people on the defensive. It is better to state what they were doing and ask how they can put it right in future. Consider 'showing them' what they were doing by role playing or acting out what they did rather than telling them.

"Do you mind if I show you what I saw you do when you walked in?"

iii) Wrap up

"Now I know you had your reasons for being late but can you see why I can't have that in the lesson? "

"What could we do next time?"

"Is there anything I can do to help?"

"Is there anything you want to say?"

"Thanks for your time"

Following up in this way helps build relationships; it reinforces the fact that we are there to help and support them – but also that we always follow up on rule breaking.

Problem #7:

Won't complete work in class

Once a student has actually made a start on their work it's clear that at least two of the big demotivators - fear (of looking a failure or of appearing to be a 'goody two shoes' in front of under-achieving peers) and inadequacy (feeling they lack the necessary skills to bother attempting the task) – no longer have influence. They've made a start on the work so something has gone wrong along the way.

It's a bit like starting off on a journey and then deciding you don't want to continue. You've gone to the trouble of packing your bag and getting in the car but then decide to pull over half way down the motorway. Was there too much traffic? Did you forget something and decide to concentrate on that instead? Did something go wrong with the car? Did something at the side of the road distract you? Did you get too tired and need a snooze? Did you decide to pick up a hitch-hiker and go off somewhere else? Or did you simply decide the destination probably wasn't somewhere you want to visit after all?

When students' efforts tail off during a lesson after the work is started it's probably down to one or more of the following:

• Being distracted by other students or outside interruptions.

• Losing interest in work that becomes repetitive or too easy.

• Getting frustrated with work that becomes too difficult. (If they aren't gaining a sense of achievement they will soon switch off – remember how important 'empowerment' is?)

• Something going wrong with the equipment they're using which breaks their concentration and takes them out of 'work mode'.

• Discomfort – is the room too warm and stuffy? Is it too cold? Is there a bad smell floating around? (If you're teaching teenage boys it's highly likely).

• Waning energy, becoming lethargic.

• Finding that other students are getting all the attention. (They may feel the need to switch off/act up to get some negative teacher attention if they see other students taking up the teacher's time by doing so).

As you can see there are plenty of possible reasons for a student tailing off in a lesson. This list is by no means exhaustive, but each of those possible reasons has one thing in common – they can all be alleviated or prevented with good planning. This is one area of motivation in which the teacher has a considerable amount of control. Getting them to start work is the biggest problem and once they've actually made a start, keeping them working can be achieved simply by pre-empting the reasons above.

So how do you plan ahead for students who lose their motivation to work during lessons despite having made a reasonable start?

1. Take efforts to minimise and prepare for distractions. Distractions can take many forms – some avoidable, some not – but there are ways we can reduce chances of occurrences and minimise their effects. Here are a few common distractions and ways to deal with them:

Distraction #1: Farting: Some boys (and rugby-playing girls) seem to take great delight in farting during lessons, usually when everyone in the room is silent for extra comic effect. We can't control what he eats beforehand but we can reduce the chances of this happening by giving the boy sufficient attention so he doesn't feel as much need to cause a disruption; but we should also have a good plan in place to deal with this particular distraction when it does occur.   Iron-clad consequences are the best way...

Teacher: *Tommy we don't do that in lessons. Please pack up your things and move to the seat at the back. If it happens again you'll go to Time Out (or come back at break for five minutes – whatever sanction you have in place.)*

Tommy: *I couldn't help it.*

Teacher: *That may be true Tommy but it's something we have to learn to control. Move now please or, as I said, you'll be going to Time Out.*

The trick, as with any confrontation like this, is to show as little emotion as possible, not get drawn into a discussion or argument and to follow up EVERY time.

If you don't know who the culprit was you use a slightly different plan. Open a window, show as little concern as possible and tell students who are overreacting to be quiet and stop being silly. Have an activity on hand with which to re-focus them.

NB// No matter how much they protest they 'couldn't help it' I would always assume it was deliberate and issue the consequence. Once you let one off for an 'accident' the rest have a perfect excuse for a repeat performance.

Distraction #2: Asking to go to the toilet: This is the favoured 'work-avoidance' strategy in many classrooms and you're going to have to have a plan for dealing with it. My personal view is that anyone can hold on for an hour (the duration of most lessons) and if they can't, they need to learn how to. I know there has to be provision made for some individuals on health grounds but unless they have a note from parents and/or the school has been made aware of this problem, all students are treated the same. They are given opportunity to go to the toilet before the lesson starts and then nobody goes during the lesson. If that's too draconian for you, you can try being lenient on a student who claims they about to 'wet themselves' and then come up with another plan to deal with the five students who say they have the same problem ten minutes later. It is better to have one rule, and stick to it.

If you're worried about denying students their rights and receiving formal complaints from parents there are other alternatives such as issuing 'toilet passes' or setting a limit of one toilet visit per lesson per student, and recording visits in a file or the back of the student's book. In each case the student should be given a definite time by which they should be back in the room (written in their book/on the card) and they should take this with them. This will enable other staff such as tutors and other teachers to monitor trends – as well as preventing the student from being wrongly accused of wandering if caught in the corridor.

Distraction #3: Peers. This is easy to prevent and deal with. Separate students who are likely to distract each other. Move the liveliest students to the front of the room so you can keep a close eye on them. Have back-up/alternative lesson tasks on hand to re-focus students who lose concentration.

2. Plan for students getting bored or frustrated. Have frequent changes of task (every 15-20 minutes – less with low ability groups) and/or increasingly higher levels of challenge for able students, with simpler alternatives for less able. Prepare tasks which meet different learning styles and know your students so that you can offer them targeted work which is likely to introduce quick 'teach-back' and discussion activities to break monotony. Remember, once they switch off, it's going to be tough getting them switched on again – you must plan ahead and pre-empt boredom. Look for the warning signs and as soon as they show the slightest waver act quickly to keep them on task. That's the time to change the activity, have a quick energiser or just offer them some quiet encouragement or support.

3. Make sure equipment is working properly and that you are able to quickly remedy it if something goes wrong. Have spare photocopies, pens, a back-up demonstration (or a technician on stand-by), calculators, batteries, discombobulators (applicable only in lessons on discombobulation) - in fact, spare versions of all the materials and equipment the students are going to be using. When something goes wrong you want to be able to just hand them a solution without a pause.

4. Make sure the room is comfortable. Ensure that you are able to control things like temperature; ie that you know how to alter the lighting/use the air conditioning.

5. Have a resource bank of energisers and fill-in activities. You need a stock of these – good, fun fill-ins and active energisers which students enjoy – as a means to get them on their feet and quickly inject some oxygen into their lungs. You have no control over their sleeping habits or the fact that Jonny was up until 4am playing on his Xbox and can barely keep his eyes open... but you can inject some energy and liven him up a bit every fifteen or twenty minutes with a quick energiser. You can find plenty on Google or in our lesson activity pack Needs Focused Lessons (which I will take every opportunity to plug purely because you – and your students - will LOVE it!)

6. Keep them on task with encouragement and praise. I've mentioned this a lot elsewhere so I'll not go into it too much here, other than to repeat that this is one of your most powerful tools – when it is used right. Remember firstly that your words of encouragement must be sincere and that many of your students respond better to quiet, private encouragement. Enough said.

Problem #8:

The disruptive joker

The joker is desperate for attention. His smart remarks, rude comments, smutty gestures, witty retorts and wisecracks may be funny (unfortunately, some class comedians really are!) but they are often a smokescreen to mask frustration, disappointment and low self esteem.

1. Make sure they know the extent of the problem. Often this child won't be aware of the problem he is causing and thinks everything is okay because he's getting a few laughs. Having it explained in private that he is actually starting to annoy the majority of his peers can have a dramatic effect on him – because this is the opposite of his desired effect. Impress upon him that he may well be turning students against himself by acting in this way and that you don't want to see that happening. Tell them you have a nifty set of consequences which you will implement with the sole intention of helping him kick his silly and disruptive habit.

2. Explain your nifty set of consequences. Make sure he knows exactly what will happen if he continues disrupting the lesson. Be sure to tell him this is not a personal vendetta against him – it's the only way you know to help him remember how to behave in lessons. Ask him if he knows of other ways.

3. Show no emotion when dealing with him. Because of the dire craving for attention the last thing you want to do is reward the joker with an outburst, regardless of how many of your buttons he has pressed. The best response is to issue one of your nifty consequences - calmly and without any fuss at all – every time he acts inappropriately. Don't give in to his protests either – just take the wind out of his sails with the following lines:

"I've told you what is happening, you made your choice. If you want to talk more about this we can do it later; come and see me after school, I'll be in my room. Now get on with your work."

...and then turn your back, click your heels and march off into the sunset.

4. Remember the positive alternative. Don't forget this student is desperate for attention so you should be ready and eager to pay some out – but attention of your choosing, and only when they do something right. Lump as much attention as you can possibly muster when they are settled and working – throw confetti, bring in a brass band... but only when they have deserved it. If you can stick to the 'no attention and no-fuss consequence' for inappropriate behaviour and 'immediate sincere attention' for the right behaviour you can see miracles occur surprisingly quickly.

5. If all else fails. Call Batman.

Problem #9:

They don't hand in homework

Homework is a typical problem with students who lack motivation. If they're not working in class where we can stand over them, they certainly aren't going to work at home. Here are two ways of encouraging students to complete and return their homework other than doling out a never-ending stream of detentions or making promises of certificates.

1. Make sure the work appeals to them. Homework needs...

a) ...Sufficient challenge - To give a sense of pride and accomplishment when finished.

b) ...Interest and a practical use - With competitors like television, facebook, games and friends, if they see no point in it or if it's dull it won't get done.

c) ...Achievability – Ideally it should be continuation of class work so they need to know how to do it. They need to know exactly what they're aiming for and what the finished product should look like. There's no point in giving them something they haven't a clue about, it won't get done.

d) ...An element of choice – We've already discussed how powerful choice can be as a motivator so include it in homework tasks. Give them a choice of task ('any 3 tasks from the following 5') or a choice in the presentation method (produce a mind-map, report, illustration, magazine article or model').

e) ...To be written down – Always make sure students have the task written down clearly before they leave the room or post the task up on a blog/website so that they can access it any time.

f) ...Occasional group interaction – We know that students like to work together so there is some merit in the idea of occasionally (or even regularly if it proves successful) setting a project which requires students to work in groups for completion. The individual accountability from peers involved in group work gives extra impetus to get the task completed.

2. Get parents/carers involved. If you have children you're no doubt fully aware how much of a problem the whole issue of homework can cause at home. Parents do the cajoling, reminding, threatening, punishing and bribing while kids do the lying, avoiding, promising, making excuses and delaying. In many homes World War III breaks out over this single issue almost every night while in others it isn't even mentioned. However, despite what you might think, even if a particular student's home appears totally unsupportive, 'home-work' problems can be best tackled with increased contact with 'home'.

Explain to parents that homework involves the efforts of three separate parties – school, child, home – and that each party is dependent on support and input from the other two if the system is to work properly. Also be sure to explain that the sole purpose of homework is to help the child progress, succeed and do well. You don't want to come across as if this is for your benefit – why should they want to help you out?

If you have trouble getting support from some parents the key is to convince them that you are trying to help them and their child and make life easier for all of them. One of the key ways to motivate anyone is to answer the WIIFM (What's In It For Me?) question. You need to show them how a little bit of support from them is going to have a dramatic effect on their child's progress in school and consequently on home life – happier child, easier life, fewer arguments, fewer detentions, fewer requests to visit school for a 'little chat' etc.

Begin by clearly explaining the current situation; show them a record of homework tasks that have been missed and the school policy and procedure for dealing with missed homework. Show them that it is neither pleasant nor beneficial for the student. If possible show them statistics for the effect of missed homework on overall grades.

Then show them the specific things they can do to help together with the days/times when this should happen. They'll need a copy of the homework schedule showing the days the work has to be handed in together with the suggested time to be spent on a task. Setting a regular, definite block of time – say 4:30-5:30pm - helps teach them time management.

Try to encourage them to set a time early on in the evening so that a) the child is still fairly alert and b) X Factor hasn't started. The idea is to create a habit, a routine which doesn't interfere with evening entertainment too much.

Another reason to set an early time is that it enables consequences to be brought into play (see below). If homework is allowed to be last thing at night and the child is allowed to play on a computer or watch TV all night before that, how can consequences be applied?

They'll need a list of necessary materials and supplies to make available at home (in some cases the school could supply these) and you could even provide them with a set of 'parent notes' for a task the child is likely to find challenging so that they can take part and provide some assistance and instruction. I've dealt with many parents with severely academic limitations and they were delighted when I gave them these.

Finally, they may benefit from some behaviour management guidance (as mentioned above) in use of suitable consequences such as withholding TV/computer game/mobile phone/pocket money until homework is completed. The easier you can make it for them to take part, the better the chances they will.

Whenever we've done this the feedback from both the parent and the child has been very positive - parents enjoy spending some quality time with a child they have possibly had very little quiet contact with for a long time, while the students start to enjoy a sense of achievement as well as the parental contact.

Problem #10:

They don't bring equipment

This is one of those seemingly unimportant issues which is often swept under the carpet by a teacher who is frantically trying to concentrate efforts on more serious issues – like Mary and Matilda cat fighting, Liam smoking, Carl spitting on Graham's back, Steven chucking text books and Paul making lewd comments about the support assistant's chest – all at the same time. In a, shall we say, 'lively' classroom, it's easier to quickly hand out a spare pen to Kyle (who has forgotten to bring one) and send him on his way as briskly as possible so that you can bandage up Matilda and put out the smouldering fire under Liam's chair. Why sweat about the small stuff. Right?

Well, one reason we should sweat (or at least be a little concerned) about equipment and resources is that little things like this can easily trip up even the most well-prepared classroom manager if they get out of hand. Remember the comment I made above – 'what you allow, you encourage'? Every time you hand over a spare pen from your rapidly disappearing spare pen pile you effectively train your little angels that it's perfectly acceptable to come to class without one. So before long, they're all at it. Suddenly, one pen becomes thirty five, you spend half the lesson handing pens out like sweeties and you're left with a handful of chewed gunky biros and a group of kids who couldn't give two hoots about coming to class prepared.

The bottom line is that you want to minimise the number of excuses that students will have for not starting work. Let's face it, not having a pen is a great excuse to avoid transferring words on to paper, and students know this; not having a ruler is a great excuse to avoid measuring or drawing straight lines; not having coloured pens means you can't finish your illustrations, and not having a protractor means you can't draw arched windows or even measure angles.

The more time you spend sourcing, fetching, carrying and monitoring equipment and resources (you do keep a record of items you lend out don't you?) the more stressful your lessons will be, the less time you'll have to support and manage your students and the more dependent they will become. That's before we take into account valuable text books and exercise books which are taken home and never seen again. Let's get on top of this issue and make life easier for everyone.

1. Text books and exercise books – keep them in your room.
I'm sure there's some complex mathematical formula to explain the relationship between a student's general classroom behaviour and the likelihood that he or she will return a book once it has been taken home - but let's just say that with a challenging group it's not very likely at all. And it causes huge problems.

I remember being pretty lax when it came to taking my own exercise books home as a student – they just seemed to disappear once they entered the depths of my cavernous school bag, never to be seen again. I had a new exercise book in some lessons almost every week – so by the end of term there were hundreds of little books with 'Robert Plevin' labels on them lying round who knew where, each containing about three pages of work. Maybe it's just (disorganised) boys but it's a problem which needs solving if you, as a teacher, don't want all your lessons turned upside down with cries of "Miss, I need a new book".

Your best bet is not to let them take them home in the first place. Store exercise books on a dedicated class shelf. Yes, I know you have to set homework but there's nothing wrong with giving them a separate homework folder/book/file specifically for homework. And never send text books home – that's what photocopiers are for.

2. Pens and other equipment - Offer to lend them some of your equipment in return for 'collateral' such as a shoe. Like all the strategies in this resource, there are going to be some which you don't feel comfortable about using. This is probably one of them purely because it can get very smelly in a hot classroom when half the students, (usually the students who wash least frequently), are sitting with a shoe off.

Having said that, it is a very effective way of making sure you get your equipment back at the end of the lesson. Though now I come to think of it, I do still have a large collection of odd Woolworths plastic trainers; for some reason they seemed to think a new pencil was a fair swap.

3. Encourage them to borrow from each other. This is preferable to having to continually give out materials from your own stocks. Give a brief period of time at the start of the lesson for students to borrow items from other members of the class. Be prepared to change strategy if they start removing each other's shoes.

4. Use a more positive approach. With any classroom problem there are two ways of approaching it – reward positive behaviour or punish inappropriate behaviour. Rather than focusing on students who don't bring equipment, reward those who do with spontaneous light-hearted treats (such as a garishly decorated plastic pen or antique Woolworths training shoe).

5. Focus on teaching the behaviour you want to see. This is my personal favourite. I'm a big fan of methods which develop independence – give a man a fish and all that – and the more you can lead your students towards becoming responsible, the easier (and more meaningful) your job will be. Give them a checklist to take home and fill in every morning with items they should bring to school. Then show them how to use the checklist as a memory aid – "have a quick look through it in a morning and check off items as you add them to your bag."

6. Get the parents/carers involved. Inform parents that this key issue is causing great concern - explain how it is impacting on the child's progress in other lessons and its importance as a life/employment skill. You could also mention that unorganised teenagers tend to lack the ability to move out of the parental home and often end up living their well into their thirties. That usually gets them listening. Show them the checklist you've created and ask them to remind the student each morning/evening to use it.

7. Be prepared. Always have a complete box of materials and equipment on your desk – your 'Resource Box'. Cut out the tendency for students to keep/borrow/forget to give back/steal your materials by having them clearly and boldly marked. Pink nail varnish tends to be a good deterrent if you're lending materials to boys.

8. Keep a clear record. A great way to impress students with the impact of their actions is to give them a clear picture of how significant a particular problem is. A chart provides a clear record, for both teacher and student, of how many times materials have been forgotten. It also gives a definite starting point from which to improve:

"Nathan, you have forgotten your materials every day this week, let's see if we can get one positive mark on the chart tomorrow shall we?"

Assignment 5

Well done! You made it to the end of **MOTIVATE The Unmotivated.**

Now that you have finished reading the book you will almost certainly have discovered some new strategies to try out in the classroom to get your students involved and change their attitudes towards lessons. Notice I said 'some'. You won't have all the answers – nobody does – but hopefully you will have added a few extra ideas to your toolbox. The next step is to USE those ideas (they're no use if you don't implement them) and to continue to find additional solutions. Now that you've made the start you will find yourself focusing on developing these ideas further, on learning from colleagues and uncovering new strengths in your own practice. That was the intention of this resource – to stimulate progress in the important area of motivating your students from within.

The case studies aren't necessarily intended for completion immediately. But it is hoped that you will come back to them over the next month or so as you work on improving motivation in your lessons. Hopefully they will help to focus you on speaking to colleagues, reading other materials and improving your skills so that you build yourself a reliable bank of strategies and resources.

Please remember also to track your progress using your Tracking Sheet.

Case Studies – Post-course strategies:

Go back to your Case Study sheets and add any new ideas and strategies that you've learned to the various scenarios.

You are now concerned with the POST-COURSE section. Please take a few minutes to look through the scenarios and jot some ideas down as to how you will tackle them in future. If you haven't had chance to try any of the strategies in the resource you may want to leave this a while but it's a good way to focus your thoughts on specific classroom problems.

I hope you found the ideas useful. If you did, please send any success stories and feedback to us using the help desk: http://www.needsfocusedteaching.com/helpdesk (I know opening support tickets is a bit of a hassle but if you do have anything good to say we'd love to hear it!)

And Finally!

"It made my naughtiest student as quiet as a mouse!"

"Thank you so much for the superbly wonderful videos! I benefited a lot from your creative secret agent method! It made my naughtiest student as quiet as a mouse! THANK YOU..."

Yasaman Shafiee (Take Control of the Noisy Class customer)

Take Control of The Noisy Class

To get your copy, go here:

https://www.amazon.co.uk/Take-Control-Noisy-Class-Super-effective/dp/1785830082/

Also, if you'd like to receive my FREE **Behaviour Tips** on an inconsistent and irregular basis via my email service, just sign up for your free book resources and you'll start receiving my Behaviour Tips.

http://needsfocusedteaching.com/kindle/motivate

These contain short, practical ideas and strategies for responding to all kinds of inappropriate classroom behaviour, as well as some handy teaching tips and ideas for improving student engagement. All this will be sent direct to your email inbox once or twice a week, along with occasional notifications about some of our other products, special offers etc.

Obviously, you can opt out of this service any time you wish but in our experience, most people pick up a lot of *wonderful* ideas from these emails. And feel free to forward the messages and resources on to other teachers (staff meetings, staff room, pop them into your Christmas cards etc.).

Just remember to look out for emails from '***Needs Focused Teaching***' so that you don't miss all the goodies.

"Thanks a million. As a fresh teacher, I find this invaluable."

"Finally something concrete and applicable in real life – I've had enough of the people who have never set their foot in a real classroom but know how everything should be done in theory. Thanks a million. As a fresh teacher, I find this invaluable."

Jasna (Take Control of the Noisy Class customer)

Final Reminder!

If you haven't already done so, head on over to the FREE resources page:

http://needsfocusedteaching.com/kindle/motivate

One more thing... Please help me get this book to as many teachers as possible, by leaving an honest review...

"I have seen nothing short of miracles occur."

> *"I have seen nothing short of miracles occur. My students' attitudes and behaviours have improved; they are excited and personally involved in their educational experience! What more could I ask? My E books have become my bible!!! I truly am a disciple!!!!! Love you guys."*
>
> ***Dawn (NeedsFocusedTeaching customer)***

Review Request

If you enjoyed this book, please leave me an honest review! Your support really does matter and it really does make a difference. I do read all the reviews so I can get your feedback and I do make changes as a result of that feedback.

If you'd like to leave a review, then all you need to do is go to the review section on the book's Amazon page. You'll see a big button that states "Write a customer review". Click on that and you're good to go!

You can also use the following links to locate the book on Amazon:

https://www.amazon.com/dp/B075GXZKV3

https://www.amazon.co.uk/dp/B075GXZKV3

For all other countries, please head over to the relevant Amazon site and either search for the book title or simply copy and paste the following code in the Amazon search bar to be taken directly to the book:

B075GXZKV3

Have fun and thanks for your support...

Rob

"...your strategies work wonders!"

"Thank you so much Rob for what you are doing for the profession, your strategies work wonders! I have never tried the 'pen' but will do next time! Seriously speaking, I give the link to your productions to many young teachers I know because they are so unhappy sometimes and they need help which they find with what you do! So, thanks again and carry on with your good job!"

Marie (Take Control of the Noisy Class customer)

Suggested resource providers

Name: HowtoLearn.com and HowtoLearn.teachable.com

Specialty: Personalized Learning Assessments, Learning Solutions, Courses for Teachers, Parents and Students.

Website: www.HowtoLearn.com

Details: Online since 1996, the brainchild of best-selling author and college professor, Pat Wyman, known as America's Most Trusted Learning Expert. We invite you to become part of our global community and closed Facebook group. Your Learning Questions Answered at http://www.HowtoLearn.com/your-learning-questions-answered.

Resources: Take our Free Learning Styles Quiz at HowtoLearn.com and check out parent/teacher tested and approved courses at HowtoLearn.teachable.com.

* * *

Name: Time Savers for Teachers (Stevan Krajnjan)

Speciality: Resources guaranteed to save you time.

Website: http://www.timesaversforteachers.com/ashop/affiliate.php?id=7

Details: Popular forms, printable and interactive teacher resources that save time. Stevan Krajnjan was presented with an Exceptional Teacher Award by The Learning Disabilities Association of Mississauga and North Peel in recognition for outstanding work with children who have learning disabilities.

Resources: www.timesaversforteachers.com

* * *

Name: Nicola Morgan (NSM Training & Consultancy).

Speciality: Innovative resources to motivate staff and empower schools.

Website: www.nsmtc.co.uk

Details: NSM Training & Consultancy provides high quality training for teaching/non teaching staff in the UK and internationally. We provide a large range of courses, expert consultancy and guidance, publications, conferences as well as innovative resources to motivate staff and empower schools.

Resources: http://www.nsmtc.co.uk/resources/

* * *

Name: Susan Fitzell

Speciality: Special Education Needs

Website: www.SusanFitzell.com

Details: Seminar Handouts and supplemental resources for Differentiated Instruction, Motivation, Special Education Needs, Co-teaching, and more.

Resources: http://downloads.susanfitzell.com/

* * *

Name: Patricia Hensley

Speciality: Special Education

Website: http://successfulteaching.net

Details: Strategies and ideas for all grade levels. Great resource for new and struggling teachers.

Resources: Free Student Job Description. https://successfulteaching.blogspot.com/2007/10/student-job-description.html

* * *

Name: Julia G. Thompson

Speciality: Educational consultant, writer, and presenter.

Website: www.juliagthompson.com.

Details: Author of The First-Year Teacher's Survival Guide, Julia G Thompson specializes in assisting new teachers learn to thrive in their new profession.

Resources: For 57 free forms and templates to make your school year easier, just click go to her website and click on the Professional Binder page

* * *

Name: Steve Reifman

Speciality: Teaching the Whole Child (Empowering Classroom Management & Improving Student Learning)

Website: www.stevereifman.com

Details: National Board Certified Elementary Teacher & Amazon Best-Selling Author.

Author of '10 Steps to Empowering Classroom Management: Build a Productive, Cooperative Culture Without Using Rewards'

Resources: https://www.youtube.com/user/sreifman (FREE, 1-2 minute videos with tips for teachers & parents)

*　*　*

Name: Dave Vizard

Speciality: Behaviour Management

Website: www.behavioursolutions.com

Details: Creator of Brain Break materials and Ways to Manage Challenging Behaviour ebook.

Resources: www.behavioursolutions.myshopify.com/pages/brain-breaks

*　*　*

Name: Marjan Glavac

Specialty: Tips on getting a teaching job (resume, cover letter, interviews); classroom management strategies.

Website: www.thebusyeducator.com

Details: Marjan Glavac is a best selling motivational author, engaging speaker and elementary classroom teacher with over 29 years of teaching experience.

Resources: Free weekly newsletter, 4 free eBooks (http://thebusyeducator.com/homepage.htm)

* * *

Name: Dr. Rich Allen

Specialty: Workshops and keynotes on engagement strategies for students of all ages

Website: greenlighteducation.net

Details: Author of 'Green Light Teaching' and 'The Rock 'n Roll Classroom'

Resources: Please join our Teaching tips community and access lots of free resources and ideas for your classroom by clicking HERE.

* * *

Name: Ross Morrison McGill

Speciality: Managing director at TeacherToolkit Ltd.

Website: https://www.teachertoolkit.co.uk/

Details: Ross Morrison McGill is a deputy headteacher working in an inner-city school in North London. He is the Most Followed Teacher on Twitter in the UK and writes the Most Influential Blog on Education in the UK.

Resources: https://www.amazon.co.uk/Ross-Morrison-McGill/e/B00G33GTEO/ref=dp_byline_cont_book_1

What people say about us

"As a PGCE student it is great to have the opportunity to pick up user-friendly and easily accessible information. The 'Behaviour Needs' course provides exactly that. In a series of amusing, creative, fast-paced sections, Rob Plevin builds up a staggering amount of practical and thought provoking material on classroom behaviour management. All of which are easily translated back in the classroom. Even if you have never had "the class from hell", there is something here for you and the follow up information from the website is laden with golden nuggets which will give you loads more ideas and interventions."

Steve Edwards (Workshop Attendee and Take Control of the Noisy Class customer)

*   *   *

"I want you to know that you have changed the lives of 40 of my students."

"What an informative day. The sessions on positive reinforcement and the importance of relationships were particularly memorable. I want you to know that you have changed the lives of 40 of my students. Thank you!"

Joanne W. (Singapore Workshop Attendee)

* * *

"...We will be inviting Rob back on every possible occasion to work with all of our participants and trainees."

"We were delighted to be able to get Rob Plevin in to work with our Teach First participants. From the start his dynamic approach captivated the group and they were enthralled throughout. Rob covered crucial issues relating to behaviour management thoroughly and worked wonders in addressing the participants' concerns about teaching in some of the most challenging schools in the country. We will be inviting Rob back on every possible occasion to work with all of our participants and trainees."

Terry Hudson, (Regional Director 'Teach First', Sheffield Hallam University)

* * *

"Thank you for helping me to be in more control."

"Rob, thank you very much for sharing your experience and reminding of these simple but effective things to do. Students' behaviour (or actually my inability to control it) is so frustrating that at times it feels that nothing can help. Thank you for helping me to be in more control."

Natasha Grydasova (*Take Control of the Noisy Class* customer)

* * *

"I am HAPPILY spending my Sat afternoon listening, watching and reading all your extremely helpful information!"

"Thank You Rob! What a wealth of excellent ideas! This is my 30th year teaching! You would think after 30 years teaching that I wouldn't need to be viewing your awesome videos and reading your helpful blog and website. However, I am HAPPILY spending my Sat afternoon listening, watching and reading all your extremely helpful information! Thank You So Much! I will be one of your biggest fans from now on!"

Kelly Turk (Needs Focused Video Pack customer)

*   *   *

"...terrific for those teachers who are frustrated."

"Great easy-to-listen-to video tips that will be terrific for those teachers who are frustrated.

I'm forwarding this email on to the principals in my district right away!"

Sumner price (Take Control of the Noisy Class customer)

*   *   *

"Many thanks for all these really helpful life-savers!"

"Very many thanks. I have given myself trouble by letting kids into the room in a restless state with inevitable waste of teaching time. Your advice on calming them down in a positive, non-confrontational way and building rapport is very timely. Many thanks for all these really helpful life-savers!"

Philip Rozario (Take Control of the Noisy Class customer)

*   *   *

"Fantastic way to create a calm and secure learning environment for all the students."

"Thanks so much Rob. Fantastic way to create a calm and secure learning environment for all the students. It's great how you model the way we should interact with the students – firmly but always with respect."

Marion (Take Control of the Noisy Class customer)

* * *

"I will be recommending that the teachers in training that I deal with should have a look at these videos."

These tips and hints are put in a really clear, accessible fashion. As coordinator of student teachers in my school, I will be recommending that the teachers in training that I deal with should have a look at these videos.

Deb (Take Control of the Noisy Class customer)

* * *

"I found Rob Plevin's workshop just in time to save me from giving up."

"I found Rob Plevin's workshop just in time to save me from giving up. It should be compulsory – everybody in teaching should attend a Needs-Focused workshop and meet the man with such a big heart who will make you see the important part you can play in the lives of your most difficult students."

Heather Beames (Workshop Attendee)

* * *

"...the ideas, strategies and routines shared with our teachers have led to improved classroom practice."

"The Needs Focused Behaviour Management workshops in support of teacher training in Northern Ireland have been very well received and the ideas, strategies and routines shared with our teachers have led to improved classroom practice. This has been validated by both inspections at the University and observations of teachers."

Celia O'Hagan, (PGCE Course Leader, School of Education, University of Ulster)

* * *

"I have never enjoyed a course, nor learnt as much as I did with Rob."

"What a wonderfully insightful, non-patronising, entertainingly informative day. I have never enjoyed a course, nor learnt as much as I did with Rob. I was so impressed that I am recommending our school invite Rob along to present to all the staff so that we can all benefit from his knowledge, experience and humour."

Richard Lawson-Ellis (Workshop Attendee)

* * *

"...since I started following the principles in your materials, I have seen a vast improvement."

"Hi Rob, I would just like to say that since I started following the principles in your materials, I have seen a vast improvement. I had to teach a one hour interview lesson yesterday and was told that they thought the lesson was super and they loved my enthusiasm! I got the job!

Diane Greene (_Take Control of the Noisy Class customer_)

* * *

"Thanks to you, students from 30 some schools are truly engaged and not throwing pencils at the sub!"

Rob, Your student engagement series has been out of this world. I've already used various techniques as a substitute and students said I was **the best sub ever.** Thanks to you, students from 30 some schools are truly engaged and not throwing pencils at the sub!"

Leslie Mueller (Student Engagement Formula customer)

*　*　*

"So often professional development training is a waste of time; you may get one little gem from a whole day of training. You've given numerous strategies in 5 minutes."

Wow! So many people have gained so much from your videos! Teachers are time poor. A quick grab of effective ideas is what we all need. So often professional development training is a waste of time; you may get one little gem from a whole day of training. You've given numerous strategies in 5 minutes. Thanks for your generosity.

Mary – Ann (Take Control of the Noisy Class customer)

Strategies List

Printed in Poland
by Amazon Fulfillment
Poland Sp. z o.o., Wrocław